China Buys the World

Andrew Collier

China Buys the World

Analyzing China's Overseas Investments

palgrave
macmillan

Andrew Collier
Orient Capital Research
Hong Kong, Hong Kong

ISBN 978-981-10-7493-6 ISBN 978-981-10-7494-3 (eBook)
https://doi.org/10.1007/978-981-10-7494-3

Library of Congress Control Number: 2017962437

Printed on acid-free paper

This Palgrave Pivot imprint is published by Springer Nature
The registered company is Springer Nature Singapore Pte Ltd.
The registered company address is: 152 Beach Road, #21-01/04 Gateway East, Singapore 189721, Singapore

Contents

List of Figures

CHAPTER 1

Introduction

Abstract In this chapter, we outline the trends in China's global acquisitions. China made $225 billion of deals in 2016, more than double the pace of the previous year. Outbound investment grew from $19.8 billion in 33 deals in 2005 to $215.2 billion in 342 transactions by 2016. That was an average annual growth of 24.2 percent—significantly above China's GDP growth. We analyze the close but complex relationship between the levels of government and corporations that determine global investing outcomes. We also provide an overview of the themes of the book, focusing on the relationship between the state and private activity, and the potential for a shortage of capital that will slow the pace of outbound transactions.

Keywords Strategies • Investment • State Grid • CNOOC • Region • ChemChina • Syngenta

A few years ago, I was sitting in my office in the Bank of China in New York when the phone rang. It was one of our bankers calling from Beijing. She was traveling to the United States and had something to discuss. Intrigued, I said sure. At the time, I was the president of the Bank of China's investment bank. We didn't make loans—that was the job of our much larger brother down the street—but we handled stock sales and distributed research on China to American investment funds. This call sounded different.

A. Collier, *China Buys the World*,
https://doi.org/10.1007/978-981-10-7494-3_1

A week later, we met in my office in Rockefeller Center. She was a rather wild-eyed Chinese woman, dressed in high style with a Gucci bag and expensive shoes. She sat down and, in a rambling speech, told me she had a client—a prospective client—who was interested in buying an American company. Could I help?

There wasn't a lot of Chinese money coming into the United States at the time. But my job was to act as the local agent for the huge parent company in China. I politely said I would be happy to assist. What was the client looking for? "He is a property developer who wants to buy movie theaters." That sounded odd to me. Operating film theaters is a very different skill than building a row of high-rise apartment blocks. I also knew that many property developers in China were expert at convincing local governments to give them good prices on land and coax banks to make loans, but generally did not have talents beyond that.

We encountered a similar reaction when we visited a personal friend who is a top New York banker with a well-known boutique investment firm. He heard our story but clearly thought we were a bit off our rocker. At the time, there was little overseas buying of companies by the Chinese apart from oil, gas, and commodities, mainly in Africa, Canada, and South America. Why would this Chinese buyer be interested in something so esoteric as the film business?

Little did we know. In 2012, the Dalian Wanda Group, the world's largest property developer, bought AMC Theaters for $2.6 billion, followed in 2016 by film studio Legendary Entertainment, for another $3.5 billion. My colleague did not reveal the name of the bank's client, but it was likely to have been Wanda. The Chinese corporate ball was rolling. And not just in the media industry. In 2016, China National Chemical Corporation agreed to buy Swiss seed giant group for $43 billion, turning a formerly small chemical Chinese company into a global giant. China General Nuclear received permission from the UK government to build an $18 billion nuclear plant in Hinckley Point, Britain, the country's first since 1995. There are many other examples.

China's engagement with the world has played out over decades, starting in 1979 with the economic revolution fostered under former leader Deng Xiaoping following the death of Chairman Mao Zedong in 1976 and China's entry into the World Trade Organization (WTO) in 2001. But in just a few short years that commitment has increased manyfold. Although ChemChina's $43 billion purchase was large and audacious, it was joining a growing tide of Chinese capital that was flooding the globe looking for an outlet, like a river overflowing into the adjacent floodplains. China made

$225 billion of deals in 2016, more than double the pace of the previous year. Outbound investment grew from $19.8 billion in 33 deals in 2005 to $215.2 billion in 342 transactions by 2016. That was an average annual growth of 24.2 percent—significantly above China's GDP growth. Although there was a hiccup in 2017 due to domestic political considerations, over the span of a decade the world has witnessed Chinese purchases of mines in Africa, steel mills in Brazil, media companies in America, auto and chemical companies in Europe—all industries have become fair game for China's giant global merger and acquisition drive (Scissors 2016).

Creating Global Champions

What has caused this outward movement of Chinese companies? After all, China has been known since its membership in the WTO in 2001 as a destination for foreign firms to plant the flag. At the time of China's WTO entry, foreign investors salivated over the prospect of accessing a market with more than 1 billion customers. China offered an eager and inexpensive workforce, a government generally (with some exceptions) willing to provide subsidized land and tax breaks, and a friendly regulatory system, all designed to coax foreign firms to set up shop in China. Inward investment skyrocketed from less than $40 billion in 2001 to $124 billion in 2010 (IMF 2014). This flood of capital—which was a painful move pushed through by the powerful prime minister Zhu Rongji—revolutionized China's economy by forcing Chinese companies to adapt to new competition from sleek, global multinationals. This time, though, the game was different. China was bringing its own brand of state capitalism to bear on the world's markets—not the other way around.

But China's corporate expansion has not occurred without costs. There is opposition among many nations to China's acquisition binge. Westerners and citizens of other countries alike are concerned about the impact of China's global purchases on their corporations, consumers, and even their governments. These concerns include the following:

- **Government Control.** Political leaders are worried that many purchases are not commercial but are done at the behest of Beijing. China's economy is dominated by state-owned companies. These issues make a difference if a country is deciding whether to hand over control of a company with large market share to what may be a state-owned Chinese conglomerate. However, there is some disagreement about what constitutes a state firm. Is it share ownership? Political control? Source of capital? I will discuss this in more detail.

- **Cheap Capital**. Loans are often subsidized by the Chinese government. These cheap loans can make it easy for a Chinese company to quickly grab market share at the expense of local competitors. This is important if you run a foreign steel company facing a flood of low-priced imports. Once again, these are complex issues. What exactly is a subsidy? Is a local government the same as Beijing? Is a public company with a government investor the same as a government company?
- **Security Issues.** Are these deals driven by commercial issues or military and security goals? This goes back to the question of the "hidden hand" of government. For example, Huawei is a competitor to Cisco Systems in the important business of networking equipment. Huawei has had military backing. Is it just an arm of the government? Should Western governments be worried about granting access to key security equipment to a foreign power?
- **Ailing Infrastructure.** Many countries lack water, power, transportation, and other infrastructure, such as in Africa, or have aging infrastructure, as in Europe and the United States. In all these cases, Chinese capital is attractive. But many countries are reluctant to hand over control of key infrastructure, particularly energy and power, to one of the world's most powerful nations.
- **The Power of the Purse.** China is making many loans to less well-off countries, loans from banks and the country's policy banks. There is a concern that these loans will be used over time to give China either ownership of key assets or influence.

Most important, there is widespread anxiety about the Chinese state's involvement in economic activity. A prime example is a comment by America's US-China Economic and Security Review Commission, established by Congress in 2000 to examine the national security implications of bilateral trade and economic relations with China. As the commission noted in a 2016 report:

> The Chinese government continues to play an important role in the Chinese economy, including in promotion and approval of outbound FDI. This prompts questions about the extent to which Chinese FDI in the United States could be **motivated by the pursuit of Chinese government's objectives rather than economic interest**...Because *the Chinese government continues* to exert significant influence in the sectors it views as strategic (e.g.,

> telecommunications and autos), this leaves open the possibility that a Chinese company, even a nominally-private one, may be making an investment to further the government's goals. (Gloudeman 2016; emphasis mine)

This argument about state-backed intervention was articulately expressed by Henry Levine, a long-time former State Department official and American Shanghai Consul General. He noted the "frustration" about China's entry into the global corporate world. It's worth quoting his remarks in full:

> Frustration over China's use of industrial policies to promote Chinese companies that can compete with, and replace, foreign high-tech companies has grown substantially in recent years among US companies in those sectors and policymakers. It is compounded by the fact that Chinese companies have almost unfettered access to the US market while US companies face so many obstacles in the China market (aimed at giving Chinese companies the edge). The frustration, even anger, is real and pretty widespread.

But he added that because of the importance of the Chinese market, the American government has been reluctant to tackle these issues:

> Note that President Trump has backed away from designating China as a currency manipulator, dropped discussion of a 45 percent across the board tariff on Chinese products, postponed a decision on the 232 cases on steel and aluminum (not solely aimed at China but involving them heavily) and taken only a very timid decision a few days ago merely requesting "a study" to see if a 301 investigation of Chinese forced tech transfer policies is warranted. Not the path of a President who really felt the US was in a life or death economic struggle with China would be likely take…
>
> …And, by the way, the same companies that are so (justifiably) unhappy with Chinese policies (also justifiably) do not want a trade war or ratcheting up of tensions that would put their current (usually profitable) operations in China in jeopardy. Further, there are lots of non-high tech US companies operating in China that are not feeling the impact of Chinese industrial policies and that don't want to get hurt in the crossfire of a trade war. And finally, there are the US exporters (agricultural sector among others) that are profiting mightily from trade with China and which worry that an unreasonably tough US position toward China could result in Chinese retaliation at their expense. Trade/investment relations with China are not a simple story. (Levine 2017)

Where Does the State End?

Levine's concerns are all quite legitimate.

However, what is missing from many of the analyses of these issues is a more sophisticated understanding of why the Chinese are buying foreign companies. It is easy to fall back on platitudes like "government control" or "market share." Some books even rely on government websites in Beijing for an explanation of Chinese motives. Others merely fall back on casual statements about "Chinese expansionism." What is tougher is detailing more precisely *who* and *what* is behind this mountain of Chinese cash—and how these internal Chinese motivations will play out on the world stage. Here, we intend to dig a little deeper.

To that end, this book will attempt to clarify the underlying motivations of China's international corporate push and the actors behind it. This includes the following.

- The corporations, private and public, and their leaders, conducting these transactions.
- The governmental agencies responsible for regulating offshore transactions.
- The financial institutions, including banks and shadow banks, that provide the financing.
- The leadership that sets the overall policy for China's overseas drive.

This is not an easy task. China has an opaque political and financial system. Government bureaucracies, such as the country's ruling State Council, do not trumpet their decisions. Nor is there a parade of investors that companies must solicit for their approval before embarking on a major international acquisition, opening the door to the decision making that outside analysts can delve into.

One of the key points I make in the book is that often there is no "China" that is behind a transaction. It's a melting pot of competing interests. Many of these deals are the result of intense jockeying between a number of corporate, governmental, and financial institutions, each with their own agenda. These internecine battles are rarely public. This competition is not often discussed in the context of China's international operations.

The same is true in the West—but to a much smaller degree. When Google buys a company, it will enlist investment banks as consultants, along with lawyers, and accountants and will eye its competition before announcing the proposed takeover. Outsiders are not privy to these discussions. However, Western transactions are made public and relevant documents are filed with government regulators. The US government rarely gets involved unless the proposed acquisition runs up against a few key national rules, such as anti-monopoly regulations or those pertaining to national security.

This brings us to our other main point. We will also examine the nature of state interjection into the economy. In China, the government is ***always*** involved in one way or another, either through implicit approval, general policy, indirect control, capital flows, or through direct ownership. But it's not a clear-cut action the way most foreigners think. The dividing line between the state and private economic activities can be quite thin in China. I prefer to think this more as shades of gray rather than as an abrupt division between the state and capitalism. Beijing doesn't guide the country, like the man behind the curtain in the film *The Wizard of Oz*. In fact, there is an extremely blurred line between the state and corporates, and between different arms of the state, which makes it difficult even for the Chinese themselves to figure out who exactly is behind any large corporate actions and what are their motivations. One of the jobs of this book is to explain how all these component parts fit together.

Legal scholar Curtis Milhaupt of Columbia University notes that it is not enough to speak about corporates alone out of the context in which they operate.

> Shifting the focus from agency problems in individual listed firms to networks of firms enmeshed in the party-state advances several important objectives. It provides a richer understanding of China's state sector and the architecture supporting a central component of the state's economic development model. It brings the corporate dimension of China's developmental experience to bear on important recent debates in scholarly literature. It provides new perspectives on China's future path of institutional development. And it raises significant questions about the adequacy of U.S. regulatory structures in addressing investment and other market activity by Chinese SOEs, a newly important type of global economic actor. (Milhaupt 2013, p. 759)

The crux of our analysis is the nature of the close but complex relationship between the levels of government and corporations that determine global investing outcomes. Apart from relying on existing literature regarding the web of influences in state and private economic activities, I have devised an informal taxonomy of Chinese corporate control. My breakdown focuses on three parts: ***direct state ownership***, ***political control***, and *access to capital.* These three mechanisms have varying levels of influence over corporate decisions depending on the firm's political place and the nature of the transaction.

Current Political Climate

Meanwhile, there are a number of recent "hot button" issues that affect China's decisions. One of the most important issues affecting China's hunger for global expansion is capital flight. This is a huge worry for the leadership. Although China has among the largest hoards of foreign exchange in history, it is being drawn down as more and more Chinese citizens and corporates, nervously eyeing slowing economic growth and a declining yuan, move money offshore. Beijing has to juggle its global ambitions and its currency policy at the same time.

Another issue is the rise of one of the most disruptive figures in global politics in years: Donald Trump. He has made a number of statements that run contrary to the trend of global integration and for the increasing inclusion of China into the world's economies. He has threatened to impose a 45 percent tariff on imports from China, accused China of manipulating its currency, and fostered closer relations with a country—Russia—that is no friend of China's. Several Trump advisers, including Alexander Gray and Peter Navarro, have argued that the Obama administration had not been tough enough on China, including security issues in the South China Sea. China's bureaucracy has to respond to Trump.

Another important point for analyzing Chinese corporate activity is President Xi Jinping's tighter political control. This has shifted the ground for corporations used to working more on their own. They are now under a tighter leash. In a related point, China's slowing economy will make it harder for companies to obtain capital for overseas acquisitions.

In addition to figuring out the underlying dynamics, I also examine specific transactions and policies. Why is ChemChina buying Swiss seed giant Syngenta? Why did they have difficulty obtaining capital for the deal? Is Xi's One Belt One Road policy real or just wishful thinking? Is the wave of overseas takeovers driven by government policy or capital flight? Who will be the prime targets? Europe? The United States? Africa? Southeast Asia? What does the crackdown on five large companies including HNA and Anbang mean for overall corporate expansion?

Also, when relevant, I plan to discuss my own experiences as a former banker with the Bank of China, a reporter in Beijing, and an analyst based in Hong Kong. In my previous role as a journalist, I found that personal experience and local interviews lend depth, insight, and accuracy to what can be a dry recitation of facts and figures. These corporate acquisitions are in essence very dramatic confrontations between powerful people and institutions, events that will have a profound impact on countries around the globe. These interviews also provide insight into the reality of the forces affecting the corporate deals.

The book is broken down as follows. The first section includes an outline of the overall flow of acquisitions over time and the amount of capital expended, what I call the current trends. The second section contains a discussion about some of the major deals, who the figures are behind them, and why they are doing them, with a focus on one deal in particularly, ChemChina/Syngenta.

The next section examines the fuzzy line between state and non-state in China and is the theoretical heart of the book. It's no use peering into China's corporate world without comprehending the complex array of government officials—from small townships to Beijing—that write the rules of the road.

The fourth section addresses China's international strategy in broader terms. This consists of the issue of capital flight, the use of debt as a means of foreign influence, President Xi's highly touted "One Belt One Road" strategy to invest in the broad swathe of nations from China to Southeast Asia, Central Europe, and Western Europe, and security issues.

The fifth chapter analyzes the source of capital for these transactions. China often uses capital as a form of control. While many nations publish laws governing behavior, China has turned the banking system into a kind of giant baton, prodding and pushing—like a farmer herding his cattle—economic actors in the right direction. This includes the state banks, the privately controlled joint-stock banks, and a host of other so-called Shadow Banks. My previous book, *Shadow Banking and the Rise of Capitalism in China*, discusses this issue in greater detail, but many of these concepts apply to international transactions.

The last section looks to the future. Will China take over the world? Are its corporates prepared to dominate industries spanning the globe? Or is this a short-term phenomenon that will peter out when China runs out of cash or its corporates discover the difficulties of imposing a Chinese management style on the rest of the world? This is my most speculative chapter—but blue-sky opinions are often the most thought-provoking.

I come to several conclusions.

- First, there will be a tug and pull in the financial system between the poles of market capitalism and state control. Overseas recipients of Chinese capital need to understand what the state's influence is on any transaction.
- Second, Beijing will continue to promote acquisitions that forward its strategic goals, including security, technology, and raw materials. However, smaller-scale transactions, along with those among favored companies, will be allowed to proceed.
- Third, there is likely to be a shortage of capital from the formal and informal souces, shadow banck, that will make it harder for firms to conduct overseas deals.

Bibliography

Gloudeman, Lauren, and Salidjanova, Nargiza. 2016. *Policy Considerations for Negotiating a U.S.-China Bilateral Investment Treaty*. Staff Report. U.S.-China Economic and Security Review Commission, August.

IMF. 2014. International Financial Statistics. *China Outlook*. Washington, DC: IMF, December 20.

Levine, Henry. 2017. Private Correspondence with the Author, August 18.

Milhaupt, Curtis J. 2013. We Are the (National) Champions: Understanding the Mechanisms of State Capitalism in China. *Stanford Law Review*, 65: 697.

Scissors, Derek. 2016. American Enterprise Institute, July 14.

CHAPTER 2

The Setting

Abstract We discuss recent major transactions and the people behind them. These include HNA, Anbang, Dalian Wanda, and ChemChina/Syngenta, high profile companies whose ambitions have been blocked. We analyze the percent wealth that is controlled by a small elite that contributes to China's global acquisitions. We also look at the response by Beijing regulators to the outflow of capital and how Chinese corporates have redirected their strategy in light of recent restrictions on access to foreign exchange.

Keywords Energy • Raw Materials • China Foreign Direct Investment • East Asia

The Bureaucratic Entrepreneur

In the 1970s, Ren Jianxin (pronounced Ran Jenshin) was a lowly engineer in an obscure chemical factory in the dusty outback of western China. He was employed by the Chemical Machinery Research Institute in the city of Lanzhou, in the far west of China where the Han Chinese mingle with local minorities and the desert sands stretch for miles until they gradually meet the mountains of Tibet.

But Ren was ambitious. While working, he earned a bachelor's degree in mechanical engineering and a master's degree in business administration.

A. Collier, *China Buys the World*,
https://doi.org/10.1007/978-981-10-7494-3_2

But his real coup came a few years later. Ren did what many early Chinese entrepreneurs did to succeed—he found a powerful political protégé (Bloomberg February 4, 2016).

In 1984, Ren borrowed 10,000 yuan from the institute to start the BlueStar Chemical Cleaning Group. His first employees scrubbed tea kettles as Ren pursued the most reliable path to power in China—becoming BlueStar's Communist Party secretary, according to his biography. Speaking in a company video, Ren cited a woman named Gu Xiulian as a key ally—his early protégé. She would have been a formidable friend as head of the Ministry of Chemical Industry from 1989 to 1998 and for 20 years a member of the Communist Party's powerful Central Committee.

With Gu's backing, and a driving ambition, Ren launched into a buying spree that turned a relatively low-level chemicals firm into one of the country's largest. Over the next few years, he bought more than 100 ailing state firms and brought them into his own company. While this saddled him with unprofitable operations, it had a more important result: It earned him favors from provincial officials across China, the kind of senior politicians who can make or break a rising corporate chieftain with a few phone calls to Beijing. Often, when he got hold of a company that needed downsizing, he shifted workers to his more commercially successful Malan noodle chain, saving government officials from the embarrassment of layoffs.

The Party and the Entrepreneurs

The relationship between the Communist Party and the country's entrepreneurs is complicated. There has long been an intense debate among scholars about something as basic as the difference between a private and a state firm in China. Can it be defined by source of capital? Ownership? Licensing? Independence from government? For example, in the early days of economic reforms, many private companies were launched under the guise of state licenses; these were the so-called Red Hat firms. But it's unclear how independent they really were. They may have utilized private capital but obtained contracts through their government connections. Or they were backed by the local government but sold their products through open markets. The same issues continue to this day. Was Ren running a private operation or a state firm? It is pretty clear that his ability to amass a giant corporation out of disparate assets must have had strong local political support.

Whatever he did, his firm acquired scale. With revenues of $45 billion in 2016, ChemChina has become China's largest chemical company. It has more than 140,000 employees with 52,000 outside China, and eight of its companies are listed in the Chinese stock exchanges. Even with its global scope, it is still a very Chinese firm. For example, the company's website displays a list of unusual corporate goals:

- Harmony brings wealth.
- Detail is the key of success.
- Everything is good for something.
- A hedge between keeps friendship green.
- Serve the corporate world with loyalty.
- Loyalty counts most.
- The deepest disdain goes to those who forsake principle for profit.
- Cherish life, enjoy living. We don't want profits with blood.

Overseas, Ren completed his first deal in 2006, buying Adisseo Group for E400 million. It was China's largest investment in France. That followed with eight other deals in Australia, Norway, Israel, the United States, Italy, and Germany. The 2015 agreement to buy Pirelli, the world's fifth-largest tire maker, for E7.1 billion, drew attention because it put one of the symbols of Italy's manufacturing industry in Chinese hands.

But the transaction that put ChemChina on the map was the $43 billion takeover in 2017 for Syngenta of Switzerland. Companies, bankers, and investors the world over sat up and took notice. The size of the transaction, the involvement of several countries, and the sensitivity about genetically modified food put Syngenta in the middle of a global debate about China's role in corporate activity.

There was even political opposition. This was to be expected given the size of the offer and the sensitivity of control over Syngenta's genetically modified food. The Chinese offer even prompted a political backlash in the US Senate, leading to a call to change how America treated foreign acquisitions. Senate Judiciary Committee Chairman Charles Grassley (R-Iowa) made a request for the US Department of Agriculture to have a permanent role on America's key body that regulates the sale of American assets, called The Committee on Foreign Investment in the US (CFIUS):

> The ChemChina-Syngenta merger raises questions about national security because of the need to ensure a safe food supply in the United States. It's clear that China is looking at purchasing companies with food production expertise as part of a long-term strategic plan and a component of their

> national security. We need to be looking at these mergers in the same way, so it makes sense for CFIUS to take that angle into consideration when reviewing these transactions. (Grassley 2016)

Grassley introduced legislation in July 2016 that would secure USDA's position on CFIUS and ensure that foreign acquisitions of major US food and agriculture companies would be reviewed for potential national security threats. USDA had not been among the 16 federal agencies that comprised CFIUS, a panel chaired by US Secretary of the Treasury Jacob Lew.

There was even *backlash within China* against the Syngenta deal. Around 400 Chinese citizens signed a letter to protest the purchase of Syngenta by state-owned ChemChina, saying the deal would eventually lead to genetically modified crops being sown across China. "The acquisition of Syngenta and the promotion of its genetically-modified and agro-chemical agriculture in the country would destroy the country's own agriculture and food security," the protesters said in the letter, seen by *Reuters*. "They argue Genetically Modified Organism (GMO) strains would contaminate Chinese staple crops. ChemChina must immediately stop the suicidal acquisition from causing a disaster to the Chinese nation" (Shuping and Stanway 2016).

What followed next illustrated the confusing nature of power in China. The protest group sent its note not to the Ministry of Health, which ordinarily would regulate domestic food issues, but to the organization that controls China's biggest state companies: The State-Owned Assets Supervision and Administration Commission of the State Council (SASAC). SASAC is a relatively toothless organization but is the ultimate holding company for the giant state-owned enterprises (SOEs) owned by the government—and was ChemChina's ultimate master. SASAC also indirectly controls another 130,000 firms owned by Provincial or other local governments. A SASAC spokeswoman said her office had not yet seen the letter, but was looking into it. Because it appeared that the central government was in favor of obtaining technology related to genetically modified foods, there was little chance the public's opposition would succeed. There were even rumors that the protest was set in motion at the behest of another Chinese corporate, Sinochem Group, that was seeking to take ChemChina's seat at the global chemicals table. In any case, that was the last the public heard about GMO concerns scuttling ChemChina's audacious Syngenta bid.

Savvy players like Ren are vital to China's economy. He's clearly flourished as a wily dealmaker able to negotiate the thorny pathways of China's quasi-free market economy. On the one hand, he's busy wooing banks and wealthy individuals to invest in his grand schemes. On the other, he's convincing the government that he should be the one to lead the way to create a global food and genetically modified seed giant. He claims his hobby is reading the works of Chairman Mao. He certainly would need the former leader's political skills to survive in China.

Ren is a classic example of what I call the "bureaucratic entrepreneur." He operates within China's political system, dodging between the state and private sectors. Flat assumptions among Western governments that China (i.e., the state) is targeting certain goals miss the point. The goals often can be a mix of private profit and state ends. This is one of the main questions I will attempt to address in this book—where do the state end and the private sector begin in China?

But before I explore the particular world of Chinese dealmaking, let's examine the trends in the expansion of China's global corporations.

The Trends

The focus of this book is on the politics behind China's tsunami of foreign investment and acquisitions. Understanding the forces underlying China's global ambitions will help outsiders to interpret—and hopefully forecast—the future patterns of outward-bound capital. However, it is important to understand the historical pattern.

China has rapidly increased its appetite for foreign acquisitions over just a short period of time. There is a growing literature examining this trend. The problem is that China's economy, domestic forces, and changing global economic factors alter the dynamics of these investments, and thus the trends, and underlying motivations, have changed.

China's FDI

The chart below shows the actual outbound flows from 2005 to 2016. Outbound investments grew from \$19.8 billion in 33 deals in 2005 to \$215.2 billion in 342 transactions by 2016. That was an average annual growth of 24.2 percent—significantly above China's Gross Domestic Product (GDP) growth (Fig. 2.1).

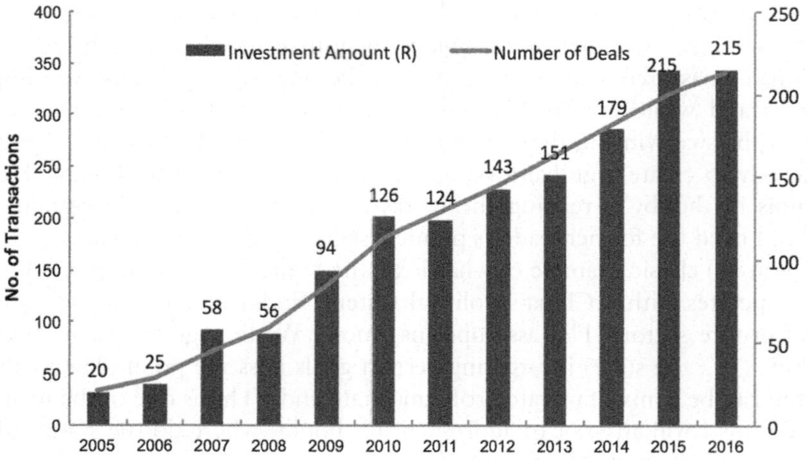

Fig. 2.1 China's Outbound Transactions. Source: American Enterprise Institute, Global Investment Tracker

However, over time, the composition of that investment changed. The chart below makes the changes quite clear; where energy long topped the list, accounting for almost 60 percent of transactions in 2010, since then transport and technology have become more important. In the early years, names like China National Offshore Oil Corp. (CNOOC), China National Petroleum Corp. (CNPC), China Petroleum and Chemical Corp. (Sinopec), China Minmetals Corp., and China Railway Construction dominated flow. Later on we see semi-privates firms like Zoomlion in construction, Anbang Insurance, internet firm Qihoo, and conglomerate investment firm Fosun (Fig. 2.2).

What caused this change? China began focusing less on obtaining energy and raw materials than on expanding its top industries. In addition, over time private sector activity in a wide variety of industries became more important. The chart below shows that energy dropped from 36.7 percent of the total in 2008 to just 26 percent in 2016. Technology jumped from 1.3 percent to 11.3 percent. Metals plummeted to 2.9 percent from 27.4 percent (Fig. 2.3).

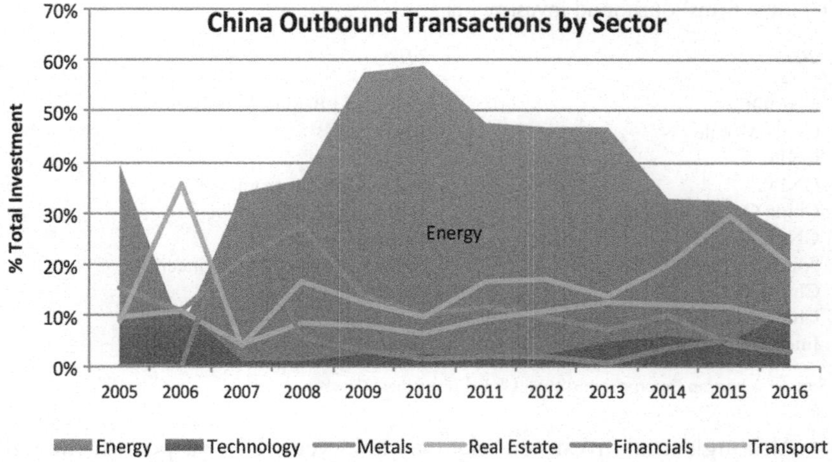

Fig. 2.2 Outbound Deals by Sector. Source: American Enterprise Institute, Global Investment Tracker

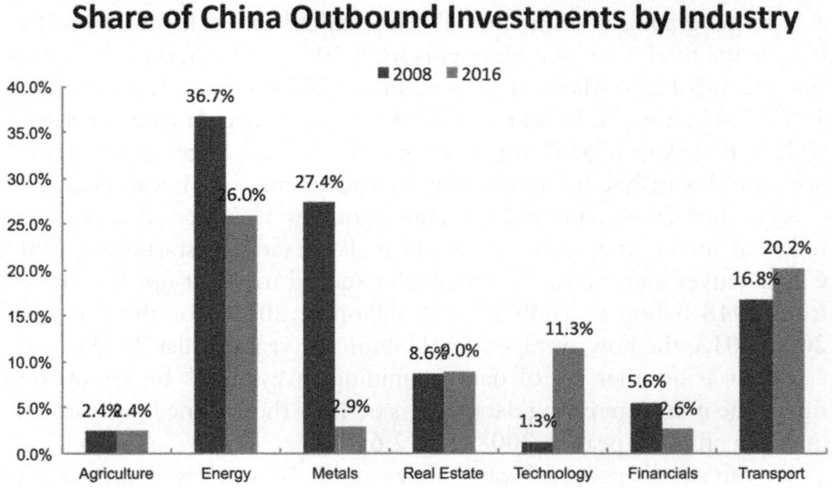

Fig. 2.3 Outbound Investments by Industry. Source: American Enterprise Institute, Global Investment Tracker

Chinese firms' outbound investments

2005	*2016*
CNOOC	Qihoo and Beijing Kunlun
China Mobile	State Grid
CNPC	CITIC
CNPC	San'an Optoelectronics
China Ocean Shipping	Shandong Delisi
CNOOC	Anbang Insurance
Southern Power Grid	Fujian Construction Engineering
Chinalco	Fujian Grand Chip
China Railway Construction	State Grid
Jinchuan	Shenhua's Watermark

Source: American Enterprise Institute, Global Investment Tracker

Although total investment skyrocketed over a 15 year period, the size of the average transaction remained relatively flat. The average size rose from $788 million in 2005 to $1.3 billion in 2008 before falling to the $800–$900 million range for the next decade. The rise in average size reflected growing confidence in international transactions, while the modest decline represented a shift from state to private firms (Fig. 2.4).

The geographical destination also has shifted through the years. If we bundle the total value of investments from 2005 to 2016, the top destination is sub-Saharan Africa, at 17 percent or $252.6 billion. Europe follows at $227.8 billion, West Asia at $224.8 billion, North America at $198.4 billion, East Asia at $192.8 billion, and the United States at $153.8 billion. But this analysis lumps together all investments for 11 years (Fig. 2.5).

The shift from commodities and resources to other industries was reflected in the geographic destination. For example, starting in 2009, China's investment in the United States started to shoot up. It increased from $948 billion in 2009 to $4.8 billion in 2013. For the five years, 2009–2013, the flow averaged $3.9 billion per year (Dollar 2015).

Below is another set of data examining investments by region over time. The most interesting datapoint is perhaps the decline in investments in Africa after the peak in 2008 (Fig. 2.6).

We can see the geographical changes in the chart below, comparing the first and last years of our data set in percentages of the total. In 2005, the United States accounted for just 8.8 percent of total overseas investments by Chinese firms. By 2016, that had jumped to 22.5 percent. Europe had

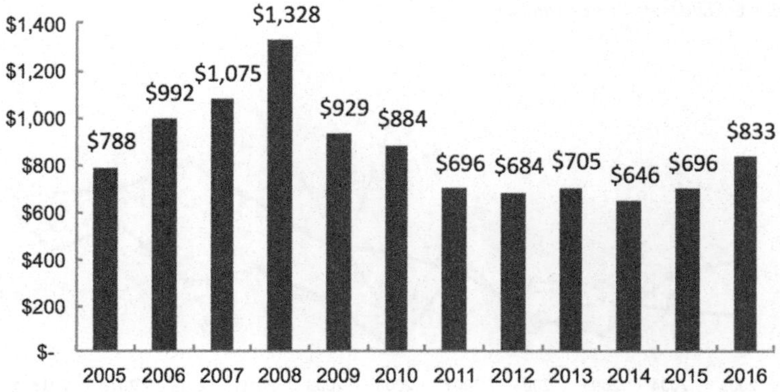

Fig. 2.4 Average Transaction Size. Source: American Enterprise Institute, Global Investment Tracker

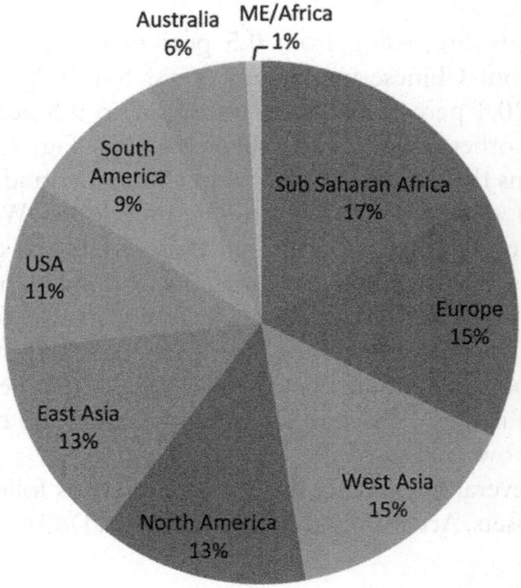

Fig. 2.5 China Outbound Investment by Region

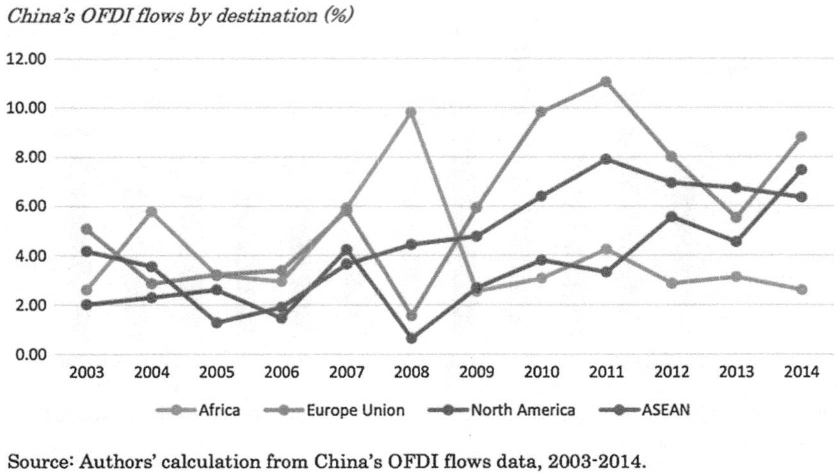

Fig. 2.6 China's FDI Flows by Geography. Source: Bloomberg

a similar growth rate, rising from 0.5 percent to 22.8 percent. Which countries lost out Chinese investment flows? South America fell to 6.9 percent from 20.1 percent; West Asia dropped to 9.8 percent from 33.9 percent. Many other regions were relatively stable (Fig. 2.7).

This confirms the widespread view that China was gradually shifting its priorities from resource-rich countries to developed Western markets. Why? First, the commodity boom had passed. China's commitment to building up its steel industry to chase the continued property bubble started to end in 2016. Instead, China believed that the future of its corporations lay in higher value-added industries. To achieve this goal, China needed to encourage its companies to develop sales channels in the West—and buy brand names. This was less expensive and time consuming than building up its own brand names.

There are several important trends that China has followed in its pursuit of global assets. According to economist David Dollar of the Brookings Institution:

1. China's Foreign Direct Investment (FDI) is strongly related to a country's economic size as measured by GDP. The larger the country's economy, the larger the investment from China.
2. A second key attribute concerns the rule of law. The stronger the country's set of laws governing economic (and other) behavior, the

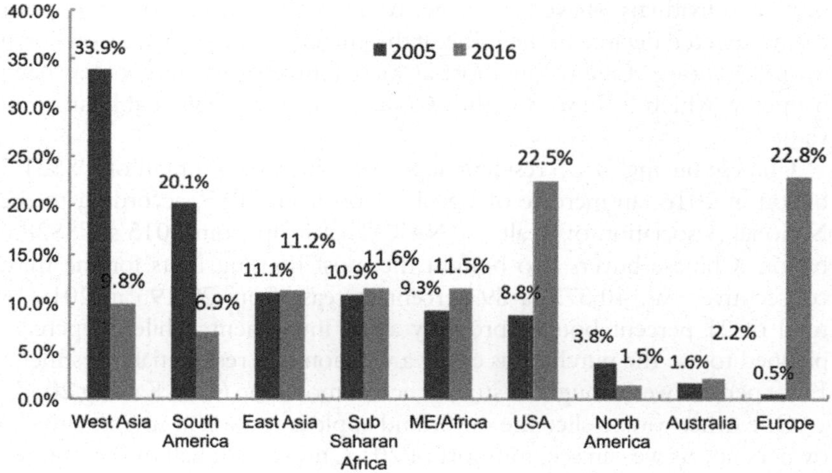

Fig. 2.7 China's Outbound Investments, 2005 and 2016

larger is China's investment. Not surprisingly, China prefers stable countries.

3. Resource extraction does not seem to be a mainstay of China's investments.

As Dollar notes, "These relationships confirm a number of common ideas about FDI: that it is trying to get close to large markets; and that, other things equal, it prefers an environment with sound property rights and rule of law. On the other hand, there is **no strong support** for the idea that FDI is primarily aimed at natural resource extraction" (Dollar 2015, p. 4; emphasis mine).

The ambition to become a major player globally by investing in developed countries is particularly true in manufacturing. First, the main investors are not the giant, state-owned firms, but private companies. As I have noted, the majority of these investments go to the advanced, industrialized countries, to expand technological expertise and take advantage of established brand names (Wang and Wang 2014, pp. 227–249).

The trend, though, once again, is moving on. Where manufacturing and high technology rapidly became the driving force for overseas deals, other issues became paramount. One particular important motivation in recent years has been capital flight. Many investors—both corporate and private individuals—have been eager to move their money offshore prior to an expected decline in the value of the currency, along with a slowdown in the economy. One of the most attractive investment targets has been property, which is viewed within China as an extremely stable store of value.

Chinese buying of US residential property hit a record high of US$31.7 billion in 2016, an increase of US$4 billion from 2015, according to the National Association of Realtors (NAR).That is up from 2015's US$28.6 billion. Chinese buyers also bought the most housing units for the third consecutive year, 40,572, a 39 percent increase from 29,195 in 2016. A total of 21 percent bought property as an investment, while 39 percent planned to use the purchase as either a vacation or a residential investment. Eight percent were bought as student accommodation (Lam Ka-sing 2017).

One other way to slice the outbound apple is to look at investments by ownership. As we can see, for most of 2017, more than half of the transactions were conducted by state companies, while 46 percent were private. However, state activity is concentrated in the resource-rich countries, while private activity has been much stronger in Europe and the North America, where firms can expand market share or take advantage of brand names (Fig. 2.8).

Fig. 2.8 Breakdown of Public and Private Investments. Source: Bloomberg

There were more changes ahead in 2017 due to a number of political, foreign-exchange-related, and other factors. I will address these in the last chapter on the future of this Chinese expansion.

Bibliography

Dollar, David. 2015. *United States-China Two-Way Direct Investment: Opportunities and Challenges*. Washington, DC: John L. Thornton China Center, Brookings Institution.

Grassley, Charles. 2016. *Grassley Statement on Conclusion of CFIUS Review of ChemChina-Syngenta Merger*, August 22. Accessed at https://www.grassley.senate.gov/news/news-releases/grassley-statement-conclusion-cfius-review-chemchina-syngenta-merger

Lam, Ka-Sing 2017. Chinese Buying of US Residential Property Hits Record High. *South China Morning Post*, July 19, Hong Kong.

Shuping, Niu, and David Stanway. 2016. China Citizens Protest ChemChina-Syngenta Deal Amid GMO Worries. *Reuters*, April 8, Beijing.

Wang, Bijun, and Huiyao Wang. 2014. Chinese Manufacturing Firms' Overseas Direct Investment: Patterns, Motivations and Challenges. *Tokyo, Japan: Asian Economic Policy Review* 9 (2): 227–249.

CHAPTER 3

The Dealmakers

Abstract Who are the companies behind China's global acquisitions? One of the largest recent transactions is ChemChina's purchase of Syngenta. This chapter looks at the financing and politics behind Syngenta, along with other top acquiring companies such as HNA and Anbang. Also included is an interview with a Chinese billionaire and a discussion of his attitudes toward outbound purchases of foreign firms. Also, there is analysis of how and why Beijing decided to restrict certain acquisitions in areas such as media and property.

Keywords Deep politics • Anbang • HNA • Deng Xiaoping • LGFV • SAFE • NDRC • Wang Qishan

Syngenta

We spoke earlier about one transaction that grabbed the world's attention: ChemChina's bid for Syngenta. It is worth going into this in more detail as it has been one of the most ambitious cases of debt-fueled acquisition—and a good indication of the strategies a "bureaucratic entrepreneur" like Ren Jianxin has to undertake in order to get a deal done in China's labyrinthine political system.

Most interesting about ChemChina's bid was the weakness of its financials. Given Syngenta's poor financial history, it is surprising that

A. Collier, *China Buys the World*,
https://doi.org/10.1007/978-981-10-7494-3_3

	2011	2012	2013	2014	2015	2016
Return on Common Equity	3.53	-6.08	-4.32	-6.17	-4.61	0.48
Return on Assets	0.3	-0.46	-0.32	-0.42	-0.3	0.03
Return on Capital	1.44	-12.51	-7.81	0.62	-0.11	2.95
Return on Invested Capital	1.14	-4.63	-2.3	0.65	0.93	2.29

Fig. 3.1 ChemChina's investment returns. Source: Bloomberg

ChemChina would take on a company many times its size. This can be explained by Ren's own corporate ambitions and his ability to maneuver within the Beijing bureaucracy.

ChemChina has not been China's strongest firm. The company has chalked up negative returns on equity (the returns based on its retained profits) for four of the past five years. Its operating margin, which is the company's profit before paying taxes, has been below 2 percent in many years, only recently creeping toward 4 percent, which is quite low by global standards. In contrast, American corporate profit margins on average range from 4 percent to over 15 percent depending on the industry (Fig. 3.1).

But the real rocket fuel behind its growth is the money it borrowed. Debt is the engine that has propelled China's global corporate ambitions—and this is especially true of ChemChina. This will be an important part of the analysis as I examine the future directions of China's merger activity. ChemChina's debt totaled 305 billion renminbi as of March 2017. It's hard to fail when you have $44 billion of borrowed funds in your pocket.

The financial backing behind ChemChina became one of the sticking points in its bid for Syngenta and another example of how even state companies have to fight for resources. Even though ChemChina is a state-owned company, the state banks were surprisingly reluctant to support Ren's Syngenta bid. There were press reports indicating that the state banks had refused to lend money for the takeover. This put a chill among investors in Europe and the United States because they felt that the lack of state bank support raised questions about the *political* backing for the deal. Hedge funds around the world that bet on the outcome of such giant mergers were busy hitting the phones trying to piece together the politics behind the money. While ChemChina had state bank loans on its balance sheet, its offshore bid failed to attract state capital. As one Beijing-based magazine noted, "underscoring the government's lack of enthusiasm is the fact that none of the four largest state-owned banks has joined" the lenders (Huang 2016).

This is another example of where the line between Chinese state and non-state actors becomes particularly fuzzy. Usually, a large loan commitment from a state bank would be a sign of approval from higher channels. Loan approvals could signal support from the State Council, the highest governing body, that usually signs off on the more sensitive, and expensive, capital investments. However, I also knew from numerous meetings with bankers in China that there is increasing commercial pressure even on the state-controlled institutions. For example, state banks have to obey government edicts on lending to favored institutions. Simultaneously, bank officials' promotions increasingly depend on making a profit. It's an awkward balance.

For this reason, in recent years there has been growing reluctance among the state banks to lend to state-owned corporations. The banks have been used as a channel for many of China's bad global investments—often to their peril—and they have been becoming more and more concerned that they will be forced to absorb losses from defaulting state firms or projects to nowhere. This explains some of the cynicism about large programs like President Xi Jinping's "One Belt One Road" (OBOR) campaign to develop trade routes to Europe. The state banks would prefer to make these kinds of loans the responsibility of the central bank, the Ministry of Finance, or the policy banks like the China Development Bank. They would rather not be in the middle of what could be a spate of bad loans.

In interviews with banks in 2016, I discovered that some of them even began to institute informal quotas for loans for official government projects such as rail. They were worried about excessive investment abroad by China Rail and other state firms for lines that would never generate enough profit to pay back the loans.

Given the pressure to produce a profit, the unwillingness of the state banks to support the Syngenta bid didn't indicate per se that the entire Chinese leadership was against the deal. It could be that the banks didn't want to get trapped in a highly risky transaction.

It even looked like there was *tacit* permission from the leadership for the Syngenta bid; I was told that it was part of an overall plan to strengthen China's agriculture sector. However, no one in the leadership was willing to put their reputation behind ChemChina. It was too risky to attach one's name to a transaction of such size, global importance, and cost that could fail. Having completed 100 acquisitions, ChemChina Chairman Ren was known as an official who could get deals done. But he also had a reputation as a person who stretches his connections and financing to the limit.

It was the classic case of giving a man enough rope to hang himself.

But what about the other, smaller banks? Would they provide the money? The centerpiece of Ren's financial support was China Citic Bank in Beijing, China's seventh-largest bank. China Citic Bank had signed a commitment for the majority of the financing, around $30 billion. But the bank also said it intended to discharge at least $15 billion to others. But to whom?

This complex financial arrangement once again further confused the question of state and private ownership of Chinese companies. While ChemChina is a state-owned enterprise (SOE), along with its main bank, Citic, much of the loan would be offloaded to private investors in the shadow banking market. Citic would do this by selling pieces of the loan to private investors in the form of China's "Wealth Management Products" (WMPs). These are....well...more or less anything the buyer will accept. WMPs were created in China about five years ago as a way for the government to suck credit out of the private sector for public investment to stimulate the economy shortly after the mortgage crisis put the global economy into a tailspin. The WMPs also allowed private individuals to increase their meager returns from ordinary bank savings accounts. Citic could bundle them with other products, or sell them directly as part of the ChemChina deal. WMPs are supposed to be transparent, but the banks have been skirting these rules. I will discuss these WMPs in more detail in the discussion on shadow banking generally. But the key point here is that Ren was very busy playing off different forms of capital to get his deal done—even without the official state banks.

In the end, the state did step in with the bulk of the funding. Bank of China became the largest backer, purchasing $10 billion in bonds from ChemChina. China Reform Holdings, a $30 billion fund launched by the central government, acquired $7 billion in perpetual bonds, and China's Industrial Bank bought $1 billion. But it was a long complicated road (Weinland 2017).

The Ultra-rich in China

Among the companies seeking their fortunes abroad, China's ultra-rich are a significant part of the migration. I interviewed one local billionaire, whose name I will keep anonymous, who made his fortune as a trader. His children have emigrated to the United States, although his major business is still in China (Author Interview May 2017).

He bought an apartment in New York for his daughter, but views this as an investment that could be sold at a later date. When we spoke to him, he was honest about his motivations for increasing his presence in the United States, blaming the difficult Chinese political environment. "It's better to move our money abroad. In China, things are so unstable. Anything the government says can have a huge influence on the market. I don't want my money to disappear in seconds. And you know what the most disappointing thing is, that even our government officials, they are transferring their assets, and sending their children aboard. How can we have confidence in them?"

However, it is clear that he has benefited from his own connections with the government. "I have super good relations with the banks. And of course, to do business, you have to develop some "guanxi" (connections) in the government. Interactions with the NDRC (National Development and Reform Commission, China's state planning board) and MOFCOM (Ministry of Commerce) are inevitable. And there are many agencies to help you deal with the red tape."

He also praised the higher quality of overseas life, including the environment—such as less smog—and the superior schools for his children.

"Nowadays, rich people in China, as long as they get the opportunities (the knowledge of how to move abroad and are able to leave), they will move, or at least their kids will. Like my daughter, it's better for her to receive an education in the USA. But I don't like living in the USA. I can't bear the food. I have a Chinese stomach. And taking the language and culture into consideration, I would prefer staying here for now."

There are a number of wealthy people in China who are in the same boat. They have managed to manipulate the political environment to their advantage and now are looking to preserve their wealth and take advantage of a better life abroad. Many of these superrich use their own companies or related firms to transfer their assets overseas.

How large is this group? I did a back-of-the-envelope calculation based on bank filings that detailed the breakdown of the bank's depositors. Then I applied this calculation to the country as a whole. I discovered that a significant portion of China's wealth is controlled by a small, powerful portion of the citizenry. According to data from the Initial Public Offering (IPOs) of several banks within China (there is no national data), I estimate that 1 percent of the population controls more than half of the bank's savings deposits. That's 15 million people with a wealth of 28 trillion renminbi ($4.1 trillion) (Fig. 3.2).

Analysis of Bank Assets Controlled by HNW in China Rmb Blns	
	2014
Total Amount of RMB Deposits	48,526
% Deposits Controlled by HNW	59.0%
Total Deposits Controlled by HNW (Rmb Bln)	28,630
Avg Deposit per HNW (Rmb Bln)	0.0018
Total HNW Customers	15,905,744
as % of China's population	1.1%
As % of China's Retail Bank Customers	11,361,246

Fig 3.2 Analysis of Bank Assets Controlled by High Net Worth Individuals. Source: Company Filings, National Bureau of Statistics

The Communist Party itself only comprises 87 million members. So the cohort that controls the majority of the wealth is most likely a subset, about 15 percent, of party members. They have access to state firms and are able to utilize channels to move capital offshore. It's no surprise that they are profiting from their connections to do so.

I also turned to another set of data from noted French economist Thomas Piketty. He analyzed a number of data sets to arrive at a figure that shows a significant concentration of Chinese wealth. Drawing from his work, for our purposes there are two major conclusions:

1. Ten thousand people control an estimated 860 billion renminbi of China's wealth.
2. More important, 11 million people control 15 trillion renminbi, or one-quarter of China's wealth. My figure is higher, but they are not far off (Picketty 2017, p. 44) (Fig. 3.3).

What does concentration of wealth mean for the future of outbound acquisitions by Chinese companies? First, there are a number of hard-to-determine variables that would affect any calculation of the impact of this wealth on international deals. Is the capital mobile? A portion of it could be in hard assets such as industrial plant or real estate that is difficult to liquidate. However, much of this may be in liquid assets in the banks. The only question is whether the wealthy can obtain permission to turn the domestic currency into foreign exchange for use overseas. The point to keep in mind is when Beijing criticizes "asset transfers"—the export of capital for little strategic value—they may very well be pointing their finger at the superrich.

	No. of Adults	% of Population	Avg Wealth (Rmb	Wealth Share
Full Population	1,063,542,632	100%	281,718	100%
Bottom 50%	531,771,316	50.0%	36,293	6.4%
Middle 40%	425,417,053	40.0%	184,173	26.2%
Top 10%	106,354,263	10.0%	1,899,019	67.4%
Top 1%	10,635,426	1.0%	8,347,004	29.6%
Top 0.1%	1,063,543	0.1%	46,156,982	16.4%
Top 0.01%	106,354	0.010%	309,247,711	11.0%
Top 0.001%	10,635	0.001%	1,623,209,327	5.8%

Fig. 3.3 Distribution of wealth in China. Source: Piketty

The Aviation Entrepreneur

One of China's biggest growth industries over the past decade has been airport construction. At the end of 2015, China already had 207 civil airports, which they hope to increase to 260 by 2020. We interviewed the chairman of a private mainland company with a revenue of 1 billion renminbi and 15 years of experience building and managing airports. The ambitious founder had completed 180 airport projects, mainly secondary equipment. Not satisfied with the company's growth, and concerned about a slowdown in airport construction as China's infrastructure boom tailed off, the entrepreneur turned his sights overseas.

First of all, he targeted an overseas acquisition, a mid-size Swedish airport construction company that was up for sale. The Swedish firm produced passenger boarding and bridge systems using a technology beyond what was available within China. This was a good opportunity for the Chinese firm to build worldwide scale and acquire foreign intellectual property. China has only one major passenger boarding bridge manufacturer, a state-owned firm, and although its products are less expensive, its quality is inferior to that of German and Swedish companies. The Swedish firm had been unable to enter the Chinese market and was seeking a Chinese company for a merger or a complete takeover. Meanwhile, the firm's domestic markets in Europe were flat or declining. There was, however, opposition from powerful, local unions, concerned about labor rights under a Chinese firm.

For the Chinese firm, the approval process was relatively easy. The company filed documents with the NDRC, MOFCOM, and the State Administration of Foreign Exchange (SAFE). Because the acquisition was relatively small—below the crucial $1 billion threshold flagged by Beijing—the approvals came through quickly.

This first generation of rich Chinese gained their wealth through hard work—along with close relations with government officials, who sign off on the big contracts, and provide lucrative connections and access to bank loans. These entrepreneurs (who I referred to earlier as "bureaucratic entrepreneurs") are not tied down by ordinary laws. As one company employee noted, "They tend to be more ignorant of rules and regulations. Business gets done quickly this way inside China."

But moving offshore is not easy for these businessmen because they have developed a set of skills that function well within the Chinese political maze but which are less useful internationally. These overseas transactions require significant amounts of capital, professional expertise, international knowledge, and experience—exactly what Chinese business owners lack. Also, since they have had to develop their business through personal contacts, as a typical family business, they don't trust professionals outside their family and are reluctant to disclose important business and financial information, which may be necessary to do large overseas acquisitions.

For internal reasons at this private airport construction firm, the deal never proceeded. Instead, the entrepreneur threw his energy into a bigger fish: building a Chinese, homegrown jet. This was the most startling plan—and a telling indicator of the ambition and naivety of China's entrepreneurs. The manner in which he attempted this bold project was very Chinese. Since he had no experience building an airplane, he had to drum up sufficient interest among the banks to back him. He found a clever way, like enlarging a photo on the side of a building, to give the appearance of size and expertise. He purchased the option to buy a design studio in Eastern Europe that had produced airplanes in previous decades but which had lost its markets and was virtually out of business. Then, with plans in hand, he went to China's largest airline, Air China, and convinced them to give him a "soft" commitment to purchase his jets once built. It was a little unclear at the time of our interviews exactly how soft Air China's agreement was. Often in China, a letter will be issued with no formal contract but that which gives the appearance of support.

Then, with his designs in one hand and the Air China commitment in the other, he approached the state banks and made the patriotic argument that China needed to construct its own aircraft and not rely on foreigners. This entire approach fits the mold of what I have been calling the "bureaucratic entrepreneur." He had spent his entire career negotiating with government officials for contracts on airport construction and services. He certainly had experience in the airport business, although it is likely that his greater skill was in dealing with the local governments. But to translate these skills into a company building jets was certainly audacious! Instead, he figured his contacts would get him to his goals.

At the time of writing, he had failed to attract enough interest from the banks to get the new firm going, which is not surprising given the size of his ambition.

The Airline Turned Conglomerate

In the world of Chinese global acquisitions, a few companies stand out. One is Anbang. A second one is the HNA Group. Chen Feng, the 63-year-old chairman, was determined to march HNA from a small airline into one of the top 100 companies in the world by 2020 that already has bought the Hilton Hotel chain and many other companies around the world.

Chen was born in Huozhou, Shanxi province, and raised in Beijing. After the end of the chaos of the Cultural Revolution in 1976, he worked for the Civil Aviation Administration of China (CAAC) and the National Air Regulations Bureau, winning a scholarship to study at the Lufthansa College of Air Transportation Management in Germany. But when he returned to China, the National Air Regulations Bureau had been abolished, so he joined the Agricultural Investment Trust of China, working with the World Bank office. This experience laid the foundation for the establishment and operation of the HNA Group. More important were his alleged political connections. Wang Qishan, the current member of Politburo Standing Committee (China's highest decision-making body), was the chief executive of the Agricultural Investment Trust of China when Chen worked there. There is much speculation that Wang has been the man behind Chen and the HNA Group—although little proof.

Chen's most famous story was how he attracted investment for the tiny startup that launched his company, Hainan Airlines. In 1990, it had only a minuscule capital of 10 million renminbi from the Hainan government. Apart from raising limited funds domestically, Chen and Wang Jian, another major founder of HNA Group, went to Wall Street in 1995 and convinced investor George Soros to contribute $25 million. Chen is known in China as a genius for raising funds, as well as an amazing storyteller whose personality and communication skills fueled his ambitious dealmaking (Fig. 3.4).

HNA is no longer just an airline company. HNA Group has grown into a conglomerate involving not only aviation, but also real estate, financial services, tourism, logistics, and other industries (Fig. 3.5).

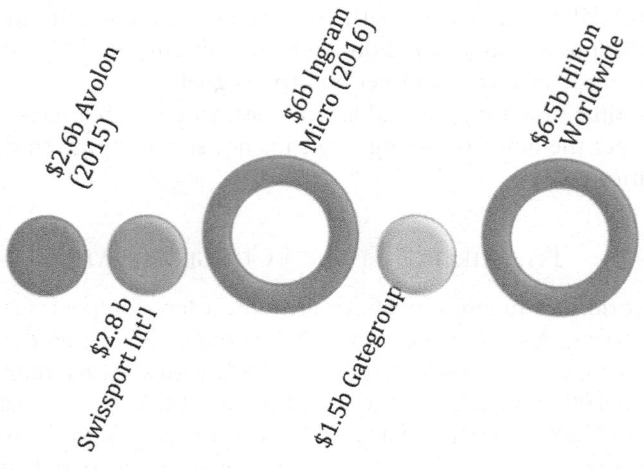

Fig 3.4 HNA's Overseas Acquisitions

But it is also famously opaque. Chen, himself, has proudly stated that no one thoroughly understands the company.

In 2000, the CAAC launched a strategic reorganization of civil aviation companies. This led to the creation of an oligopoly among three major, state-owned, airlines that swallowed up the smaller, private firms. At the time, Hainan Airlines realized that it had to expand and grow big enough to remain competitive. In 2001, following CAAC's reorganization plan, HNA took control of Xinhua Airlines and Shanxi Airlines, along with several airports.

However after a series of large acquisitions, HNA faced its own capital crisis in 2003, with cash almost running out. At the same time, SARS—a dreaded disease—broke out. Almost all the airlines suffered severe losses. HNA tried to cover the capital loss by blaming SARS, but still the downturn was fierce. A 1.4 billion renminbi loss forced HNA to rethink its strategy for survival. Its operation and profits proved to be unstable if it remained within the aviation industry. It had to extend its businesses to both upstream and downstream operations. Since then, HNA has diversified by expanding into logistics, tourism, real estate, and financial markets. During the 2008 financial crisis, HNA made further overseas investments internationally. HNA is widely considered bolder than most Chinese companies in its domestic and international expansion strategy.

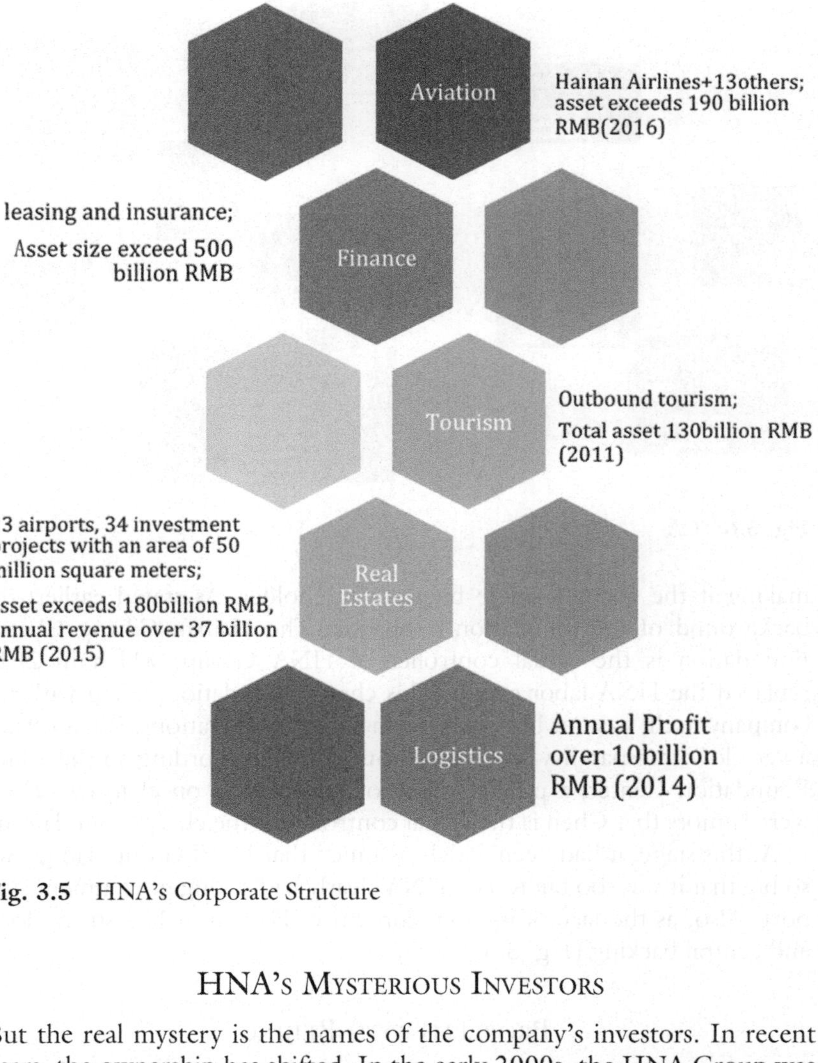

Fig. 3.5 HNA's Corporate Structure

HNA's Mysterious Investors

But the real mystery is the names of the company's investors. In recent years, the ownership has shifted. In the early 2000s, the HNA Group was 70 percent owned by the Hainan Traffic Administration Holdings, with the remainder held by Yangpu Jianyun Investment. In 2002, the Hainan Airlines Trade Union became the major shareholder of the group. In 2013, HNA donated 20 percent of its equity to the Hainan Cihang Foundation, a private foundation established by HNA Group in 2010,

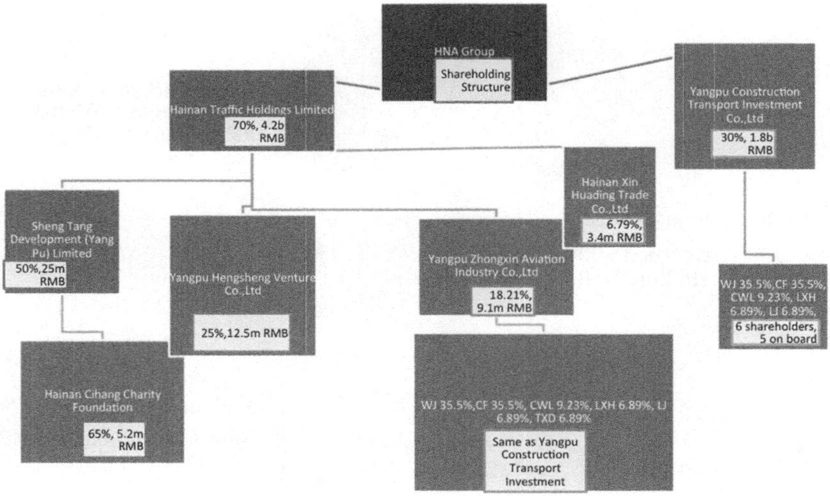

Fig. 3.6 CA

making it the group's single biggest shareholder. As stated earlier, the background of the foundation is opaque. The Hainan Cihang Charity Foundation is the actual controller of HNA Group, which in 2015 replaced the HNA labor group. This charity foundation, along with the company itself, has not been very open about its operations. It has earned a very low transparency score of 10 out of 100, according to the China Foundation Center, a public source of information on charities. There were rumors that Chen is the actual controller of the charity foundation.

At this stage, it had been widely assumed that HNA Group had grown so big that it was too big to fail. HNA clearly had strong government support. Also, as the face of its home province, Hainan, it had strong local and central backing (Fig. 3.6).

Problems with Beijing

But then the dealmaking stopped. What happened? The powerful HNA ran into the headwinds of China's capital controls. Faced with rapidly escalating capital flight, SAFE started to cancel or forbid international transactions. Concerns about possible cancellations even thwarted HNA's bids. Capital & Counties Properties Plc., a UK property developer, spurned a higher offer from HNA when it sold the Olympia exhibition center in west London to a group of German buyers in April (Bloomberg, May 15, 2017).

Still, even in 2017, HNA was able to make successful offers ranging from a nearly 10 percent stake in Deutsche Bank AG to the $1 billion takeover of Singapore logistics provider CWT Ltd.

According to *The Beijing News*, as of August 2016 HNA had 454 majority-owned and wholly owned subsidiaries across the world, ranging from airlines, to hotels and financial. It has been supported by several of the country's major banks, including a 100 billion yuan credit line from the Hainan branch of China Development Bank in 2015 and 75 billion renminbi line of credit from the Export-Import Bank of China, signaling strong support from senior circles (SCMP, April 25, 2017).

However, the company's tight government connections could become a liability. Early in 2017, China was rocked by allegations revealed by a fugitive Chinese billionaire, Guo Wengui, of corporate and government corruption at the highest levels of the Chinese government. HNA was the subject of wild online speculation after Guo said in a television interview that relatives of a senior Chinese leader, Wang Qishan, had a stake in the company. Wang was a member of the elite seven-member Politburo Standing Committee. No proof was provided.

Shares of HNA Holding Group, the owner of Hainan Airlines, recorded their biggest intraday plunge in 17 months, as investors dumped the stock after Guo's allegations. Soon after, critical news articles on the group began disappearing from Chinese websites, prompting concerns that government censors had handed down orders to delete unfavorable news about HNA (SCMP, April 24, 2017).

Guo reportedly believed that the real owners behind HNA are senior members of the country's elite. He claimed to be able to list the actual shareholders, including cousins, from memory. According to a videotaped confession by Ma Jian, a former Chinese foreign policy expert and political patron to Guo, he said he had accepted more than $8.7 million in gifts from Guo in exchange for favors, including frequent interventions with officials to cancel obstacles to his property projects. However, none of this has been proven (New York Times, May 30, 2017).

Whether HNA would survive the frontal attack remained unclear. Certainly, HNA has argued that it has good connections—but to the financial world, not in the government. In an interview with the authoritative *21st Century Business Herald*, HNA said it was able to tap its connections to obtain financing for its global acquisitions. HNA said all its deals were backed by "healthy cash flow from its core businesses."

"HNA Group has cooperated extensively with many of the world's leading commercial banks, investment banks and all types of financial institutions," the newspaper quoted an HNA statement as saying.

At the time of writing, China was scheduled to hold its five-yearly Party Congress to select the next generation of leaders. There had been significant crackdown on corruption in a number of areas that could explain the attack against HNA. Or, it could be a political wild card. In any case, HNA was obviously playing at least at the margins of the upper echelons of the Chinese government. Some would argue it had been operating above the rules.

These examples of high-flying corporates and wealthy entrepreneurs show the complex web of links between business and government in China. In some ways, they are atypical—there are many ordinary companies that flourish more or less on their own steam and are now branching abroad. However, there is no doubt that the Chinese government plays a role in many business operations—sometimes openly and sometimes behind the scenes. In our next chapter, I will try to provide an intellectual framework to the role of government in China's international corporate takeovers.

The Secretive Firm

Among the many categories of firms doing offshore deals one stands out: Anbang.

The *Financial Times* described Anbang as "one of China's most politically connected companies." The *Epoch Times* newspaper also listed Anbang as one of the five companies leading China's overseas expansion (they are Anbang Insurance, WH Group, Dalian Wanda, Fosun International, and HNA Group). They are all privately owned but well connected with the Chinese regime (Bloomberg, March 12, 2016). But Anbang, without doubt, has been one of the most ambitious.

Anbang Insurance Group Co., Ltd. was founded in 2004 and is based in Beijing. Theoretically, it is a plain vanilla insurance firm. The company provides car insurance, accident insurance, cargo transportation insurance, credit insurance, life-long insurance, and medical insurance, through its subsidiaries Anbang Property Insurance Inc., Anbang Life Insurance Inc., Hexie Health Insurance Co., Ltd., and Anbang Asset Management Co., Ltd. (Bloomberg,

Year	Acquisition
2014	Anbang acquired Belgian insurer **Fidea** from U.S. private equity firm J.C. Flowers & Co. for an undisclosed amount
	Anbang bought the **Waldorf Astoria New York Hotel** from the Blackstone Group for US$1.95 billion
2015	Anbang agreed to buy and recapitalize **Vivat**, a Dutch insurer, through the Dutch state, with transaction worth as much as €1.7 billion
	Anbang paid US$1 billion for a 57.5% stake in South Korea's insurance company, **Tongyang Life**
2016	Anbang acquired **Strategic Hotels & Resort Inc.** which owns 16 properties across the U.S. including Four Seasons resorts in Scottsdale, Arizona, and Jackson Hole, Wyoming and Ritz-Carltons in Half Moon Bay and Laguna Niguel, California etc., through Blankstone for about $6.5 billion
	Anbang purchased the German insurer, **Allianz**'s South Korea operations

Fig. 3.7 Anbang's recent acquisitions. Source: Company Statements, News Reports

March 12, 2016). It burst into the spotlight in 2014 after its purchase of the Waldorf Astoria New York hotel for nearly US$2 billion. For over a ten-year period, the company grew from a regional insurance provider to a high-profile global investment firm. But its backers were relatively mysterious—a problem that ultimately led to its downfall when its shadowy origins played against it (Fig. 3.7).

Anbang is at the forefront of China's global expansion. But it has remained shrouded in mystery, and top executives refuse to give press interviews. However, some reports have leaked out.

The real power behind the company is the Chairman and CEO, Wu Xiaohui. And the power behind him is his wife. Wu was raised in rural Pingyang county on the outskirts of Wenzhou, the famous entrepreneurial city in eastern Zhejiang province. He first worked as a low-level purchasing manager for a restaurant, where he married the daughter of a local official—his first step up the ladder.

After he moved to Wenzhou City, Wu met the daughter of the vice governor of Zhejiang, who became his second wife. During that period, he started an auto dealership business with State Administration of Industry and Commerce (SAIC) SAICMotor, where he became one of the auto firm's largest contractors. He also worked with Shanghai Standard Infrastructure Group. Both of these companies became founding shareholders of Anbang.

The year 2004 was a turning point for Wu. He married Zhuo Ran, the granddaughter of one of China's most important leaders, Deng Xiaoping, who led the country after Chairman Mao died and created the pathway to a more liberalized political and economic system. The marriage solidified Wu's connections with one of the founding fathers of China. At the same time, Wu launched Anbang in Ningbo, another city in Zhejiang province. With this strong backing, Anbang grew from a minor insurer with a registered capital of only 500 million renminbi to a global dealmaker with assets of 1.65 trillion renminbi, or $253 billion in 2016 (Anbang Group 2016). To avoid suspicion of Anbang's relation with the Deng family, Wu was said to have ended the marriage with his wife in 2015 (Caixin, January 30, 2015).

There have been a number of news reports attempting to analyze the ownership structure of Anbang. One, written by respected magazine *Southern Weekend*, was deleted shortly after it was posted, suggesting the high sensitivity about Anbang's operations.

Who are the company's mysterious shareholders? In 2004, the seven initial shareholders were SAIC, an SOE, and six other private enterprises in the automotive and infrastructure industry. They all were closely highly connected to Mr. Wu. There were seven board members: Hu Maoyuan and Liu Rong from SAIC, Chen Xiaolu, Wu Guanghui (said to be the fake name for Wu Xiaohui), Chen Ping, Yao Dafeng, and Zhaohong (Southern Weekend, January 10, 2014). Chen Xiaolu is the son of Chen Yi, a legendary former supreme commander of China during the revolution, and currently controls three of the shareholder companies. He is considered to be the prime boss of Anbang. But he denied it in an interview with *Caixin* magazine in 2015, saying he only provides consulting advice and had not been involved with operation and management.

In 2005, Anbang added four other people to the board. They were Zhu Yunlai, the son of former Prime Minister Zhu Rongji; Long Yongtu, former Vice Minister of Ministry of Economy and Trade, China's chief negotiator in joining WTO; Liu Xiaoguang, general manager of Beijing Capital Venture Group; and Dong Yibing. The fact that these prominent figures joined the company was the result of Chen Xiaolu's network.

Anbang also took advantage of its rising position by hiring former employees of the insurance industry's regulatory body, the China Insurance Regulatory Commission (CIRC). In 2013, after a series of capital expansions, Anbang experienced another big change in board seats. Wu Xiaohui became the legal representative, Chairman and CEO of Anbang, while the name "Wu Guanghui" disappeared. At the same time, a new board member joined, Liu Rong from SAICMotor, replacing Jie Zhengling. With the help of the CIRC, Anbang became a comprehensive insurance group with an expanded license.

In 2014, Anbang adjusted its board members yet again. Zhu Yunlai, Hu from SAIC, and former officials from CIRC, all quit. This was related to the Central Government's policy of "official independence" from government connections for private firms (Southern Weekend, January 5, 2014). Since then, there have been no representatives from SAIC and Sinopec. Despite several changes, core members are still consistent with the founding shareholders' group.

In the end, Anbang created a very secretive ownership structure and management. As is true for many large companies in China, it is very much directed from the top. "Strategic decisions are 100 percent made by the CEO, the team just executes," said one American fund manager familiar with Anbang. "The CEO loves to have the control position, and loves being 100 percent owner of the assets" (Orient Capital Research, May 12, 2017).

One prime example of the company's centralized controls concerns Anbang's interest in purchasing a New York building owned by the real estate–focused Kushner family. Following discussions between Anbang and Jared Kushner about the building on 666 Fifth Avenue in New York, the company went dark about its plans. Many believe that this highly visible investment with the President's son-in-law drew too much attention to China's elite, causing Beijing to pull in Anbang's reins. This was in part due to the high price Anbang was reportedly willing to pay. "What company without top political backing would even have the guts to tip their toe into 666 fifth avenue?," the American fund manager noted. "There's major headline and leverage risk by paying such a price premium" (Ibid., OCR Interview).

Anbang's ownership remains to this day non-transparent. But the government is watching.

Anbang's Thwarted Ambitions

In May 2017, the insurance regulator dropped the boom on Anbang's capital raising schemes. The CIRC forbid Anbang from selling complicated "investment products" to citizens. These had provided the flame for Anbang's global expansion. "If Anbang can't sell over bank counters, other channels can hardly contribute revenue in a meaningful way in the next few months," said Steven Lam, a Bloomberg Intelligence analyst (Bloomberg, June 27, 2017). How had Anbang transformed itself into an investment bank? It is now time to take a step back and look at the method by which mild-mannered and sleepy insurance companies grew so quickly into acquisitive conglomerates.

China's $586 billion stimulus package in 2009 led to the establishment of non-bank lending known as shadow banking. These flows were channeled primarily (although not exclusively) through two institutions: banks, which sold WMPs to individuals, and trusts, which acted like quasi-banks by pooling funds together from individuals and corporates. These were called shadow banks because they operated without many of the rules that the banks had to obey. Many of these pools of capital were invested in local government projects in infrastructure and property. This capital also helped to fill a fiscal gap in their revenues. However, over time, Beijing attempted to restrict the flow of funds from the banks and trusts to local governments, concerned about the rising debt.

Almost unnoticed, the insurance industry stepped in to fill the gap. In 2014, investments in alternative investments by China's insurance industry grew at more than double the rate of traditional investments in equities and fixed income to reach 2.3 trillion renminbi. Much of this ended up in local infrastructure and property projects. This became a new channel for shadow banking. The increase partly reflected reluctance within the leadership to use state funds to address a slowing economy. This led Beijing to find other asset pools to use as stimulus measures. This policy is similar to the US government backing of Fannie Mae and Freddie Mac prior to the 2008 financial crisis to support low-income mortgages without relying on funds from the US Treasury. There were no short-term fiscal costs to the government, but there were long-term risks to economy. In addition, the local governments actively encouraged the insurance funds to invest in their pet projects. Anbang was looking for higher returns, and local governments sought capital. "It's a great opportunity," the head of one insurance firm told me over drinks in Shanghai (OCR, May 2015).

The insurance industry's growth came through the use of alternative investments. Alternative investment refers to investments apart from easily tradable instruments or cash, like bank deposits, bonds, and stocks. In China, these are mainly composed of debt investments (infrastructure) and customized trust plans (infrastructure and the property market). This is a very creative form of financing—and highly risky—because in the wrong conditions they can be hard to sell and can plummet in value very quickly.

Although the investment horizons of these two areas are different, the expected interest rates are the same, around 6 percent. Given alternative investment's higher returns than from the typical bond, along with lower volatility than equity products, these products gained share over typical stocks and bonds among the average wealthy Chinese investor. At the beginning of 2014, alternative investments only accounted for 18 percent of the insurance industry's investment portfolio. By the beginning of 2015, their share climbed 6 percentage point to 24 percent. In contrast, the investment in bonds declined 6 percentage points from 44 percent in January 2014 to 38 percent in January 2015. Even the booming stock market failed to attract insurance investments, which slightly increased its portion of total investment by just 1 percentage point.

In general, insurance companies invested in the debt of infrastructure projects of local government or local government financing platform (LGFV) as a way to provide capital for cash-strapped local governments. LGFVs are off-balance sheet companies that were established in local towns across China as a means to avoid lending caps to governments for infrastructure investment. These investments reached a peak during China's stimulus in 2009. One of our interviewees, who was working for the business promotion office at a Jiangsu province LGFV, said insurance investments had been promoted by provincial officials to meet the financial needs of their infrastructure projects, because of the following reasons:

1. Insurance companies have stable long-term sources of funds, which match the five-to-ten-year construction period of infrastructure projects. In other words, insurance funds have maturity match with infrastructure projects and are less costly than bank loans.
2. Insurance companies were willing to lend capital at lower interest rates than trust funds, namely, 7.5 percent, according to estimates provided by an official at a large domestic insurance company. "Most importantly, unlike trust companies, we don't have any other

> implicit costs," an insurance executive told us during an interview. By this he meant it was fairly easy to raise the money (OCR, June 2016). Trusts often have to pay additional fees to banks and other third parties.

As opportunities for high returns from traditional markets declined, the insurance industry's appetite for risk grew. Anbang—and other insurance companies—realized they could raise capital the same way, by selling an investment product, and use the capital to invest not just in domestic projects, but in overseas assets, too. And that's what they did.

Anbang's Cash Squeeze

Whether it was the insurance industry's new, and risky, financial policies or the shaky financial foundations of the company, Anbang soon found itself under the hot glare of Beijing's regulators.

In June 2017, Wu Xiaohui was barred from leaving China and was reportedly under investigation by the insurance regulator. According to the *Financial Times*, a senior executive of a state-owned company said, regulators "want to stop financial institutions from doing crazy things" that might provoke a financial crisis (Financial Times, June 2, 2017).

What exactly was the problem with Anbang—and by extension the insurance industry's—funding structure?

The short-term nature of its investments left Anbang open to a shortage of cash if too many of the customers sold out. For example, in 2015, Anbang sold 47.6 billion renminbi of a product called Longevity Sure Win No. 1. The WMP offered a 4.7 percent return for one year, which would rise to 5.8 percent if the customer held on to it for additional three years. There were multiple problems. First, a one-year product would be a mismatch for a longer-term investment. In addition, it wasn't at all clear where Anbang was investing the capital. Which projects? For how long? How much was in alternative assets and how much in straightforward stocks and bonds?

The free-for-all financial attitude by Anbang was all too common among many in the Chinese insurance industry. Oddly enough, most of this free-for-all regulatory attitude was encouraged by the government, primarily one man: Xiang Junbo, Chairman of the CIRC. He had explicitly told the insurance companies to bulk up financially, invest in alternative assets domestically, and even become global investors. Following his arrival at the head of the institution in 2011, assets held by Chinese insurers nearly tripled from 6 trillion renminbi in 2011 to 16 trillion renminbi in 2017. Premiums from just one policy alone—universal life insurance—jumped tenfold from 133 billion renminbi in 2015 to 1.18 trillion renminbi in 2016. The ambitious Xiang allowed insurers to raise the limits on investments in companies, increasing their average returns from 5 percent to 7.5 percent (Caixin, April 11, 2017).

Spotting the opportunity for quick profits, new companies entered the field. Between 2011 and 2017, 41 insurers obtained licenses to become insurance firms. Although a single shareholder was barred from holding more than a 51 percent stake, these investors used relatives as proxies to gain 100 percent control (Ibid., Caixin).

While at the time of writing no insurance firm had collapsed, Xiang's lax regulatory style—and possible corruption—finally brought him down. In early 2017, the Central Commission for Discipline Inspection (CCDI) said Xiang was being examined for "serious violations of party discipline," a statement generally referring to corruption. He was stripped of his post in April 2017. He was the most senior regulatory official to be accused since the start of Xi's anti-corruption campaign in 2012.

Whether it was the investigation of Xiang or the problems at the company itself, Anbang soon saw a rapid decline in the amount of money it was obtaining from its client base. Shortly after the twin investigations, in April 2017 Anbang earned only $218 million, down from $5.92 billion in April 2016. A *New York Times* headline is an apt explanation for what happened to the beleaguered company: "Why Did China Detain Anbang's Chairman? He Tested a Lot of Limits" (New York Times, June 15, 2017).

However, China is reluctant to slow the sluice gates of shadow banking money. Although there was a severe crackdown on capital expansion and overseas acquisitions, insurance executives began planning on another boom year in 2018—courtesy of a more relaxed investment environment. According to *Bloomberg News*, the CIRC hinted that it would allow insurers once again to expand their operations. "Regulators have signaled to insurers that they will relax restrictions on overseas investment next year," said the chief financial officer of a large Chinese insurance group. "It has been very hard for us to get quota to invest overseas during the past year," said Chen Yijiang, head of investments at New China Life Insurance, one of China's largest life insurance groups. "But the pressure on foreign exchange has eased this year. [Because of that] we believe the regulators will make it easier for insurance companies to allocate overseas next year" (Bloomberg, June 29, 2017).

The CIRC permitted insurers to invest up to 15 percent of their assets to overseas acquisitions. By the end of 2016 they had invested just 2 percent, giving them plenty of financial capacity for expansion.

With the former Anbang chairman under investigation, along with the simultaneous investigation of the CIRC, at the time of writing, the outcome of Anbang's global ambitions had not been concluded. But it has been clear that the expansion of China's insurance firms would be subject to the push and pull of government edicts in Beijing.

Bibliography

Huang, Kaixi, et al. 2016. *In Syngenta Bid, ChemChina Follows Buyout Formula.* Beijing: Caixin.

Picketty, Thomas. 2017. *Capital Accumulation, Private Property and Rising Inequality in China, 1978–2015.* Working Paper 23368. Cambridge, MA: National Bureau of Economic Research. April.

Weinland, Don. 2017. Chemchina Edges Closer to Sealing Syngenta Deal. *Financial Times*, May 31, London.

CHAPTER 4

State or No State?

Abstract In this section, we analyze state control in China and what it means for other countries. We also attempt to understand how the Chinese government classifies state firms. We explore the concept of "networked SOEs" in a Chinese context to understand the relationship between state corporates and the state. We also provide an overview of state capitalism in China in general. We devise and outline our own analysis of power as it affects outbound FDI by Chinese firms using an informal taxonomy according to direct state ownership, political control, and access to capital.

Keywords Xi Jinping • Laos • One Belt One Road • CFIUS • SASAC • Congress

Many nations are warily eyeing China's global expansion. One of the most pressing questions is how much Beijing is in charge of this international corporate takeover. Is this all part of a master plan driven by the leadership in the compound at Zhongnanhai near Beijing's Forbidden City? Or is this a more random event driven by capital flight, declining GDP, and growing domestic political instability?

The conventional wisdom holds that Beijing controls the financial support, management, and strategy for the entire economy. Thus, almost any acquisition is viewed as guided by the will of the state and should be treated as an extension of government policy. The reaction among other

A. Collier, *China Buys the World*,
https://doi.org/10.1007/978-981-10-7494-3_4

countries, therefore, should reflect the realities of Chinese state power and goals. As McKinsey China noted, "There is a persistent suspicion that somewhere in Beijing resides a collective brain that directs Chinese companies' actions – and that the recent outbound acquisitions have been directed by this pervasive government planning" (McKinsey 2017).

State Capitalism

But this view increasingly is outdated. Due to a myriad of factors—including China's growing private economy, sources of capital from the shadow market, and a surprising laissez-faire attitude in the government—the Chinese government is not always driving the train. As McKinsey noted, "the extent to which they drive corporate decisions, however, is greatly overstated. Central government sets an overall policy framework, and managers of state-owned firms are rewarded in career progression for advancing it, but they are acutely aware that they are responsible for their own decisions" (McKinsey 2017).

Invariably governments, through regulation, direct oversight, or public policy, *influence* firms—the question is to what degree. This is where the discussion gets messy. Academics and economists have long debated the complex issue of where the Chinese state ends and private activity begins. Can it be described by equity ownership? By board management? Political control? Source of capital? Canada leaves their definition so open ended that it's prone to many interpretations. Canada defines a state-owned enterprise (SOE) as "an enterprise that is owned, controlled or influenced, directly or indirectly by a foreign government" (Giorno 2012).

I have seen the "gray area" many times in the course of my work as an investment banker with the Bank of China (BOC). I sat in on many discussions in China about making loans to corporations based on profitability. However, this metric frequently fell by the wayside if there was a hint of government connections. For example, I accompanied my colleagues at the BOC to the headquarters of a leading provincial investment firm, responsible for hundreds of millions of dollars of investments in everything from highways to waterworks. I had been told that BOC was under orders from Beijing to be strict about examining a company's books to make sure they had adequate cash flow to repay loans. After the meeting—one of the more arrogant CEOs I have spoken to—I walked outside with my colleagues. "Will you lend to them?," I asked innocently. "Of course we will," my colleague answered. "We'll give them anything they want—they're owned by the provincial government."

However, apart from this obvious example of direct government ownership, there are many other types of relationships that affect the status of a company in China and its access to capital. As one academic analysis noted, "Does a foreign SOE act as an independent enterprise for commercial interests or as an agent of the foreign government pursuing political interests…If a foreign SOE's governance structure demonstrates independence of its home country government, the SOE will be more likely to obtain regulatory approval and public support in the host country" (Lin 2017a).

Drawing the Line

Economists have struggled to create a dividing line between the state and private activity in China. In "Markets over Mao," the Peterson Institute's Nicholas Lardy argues that private activity has gradually overtaken state-controlled firms, contrary to the popular belief that the leadership under President Xi Jinping has increased state ownership. His analysis relies primarily on quantifiable measures of profits, revenue, and return on assets of state and private firms, a distinction accorded by ownership (Lardy 2014).

Others have contested Lardy's views. Instead, they argue that state control is wielded through many forms, not simply ownership of state firms and the profits they generate. A group of authors published a rebuttal of Lardy's work. As one commentator, Kellee Tsai of the University of Hong Kong Science and Technology, noted, "The scope of state intervention in China goes beyond familiar levers of the East Asian developmental state… In studies of comparative capitalism, state capitalism is an analytical category that describes the hybrid organization of an economy by delineating the political motives, institutional scope, and intended effects Asia policy of state intervention" (Tsai, Kellee. Book Review 2015). This is a sophisticated way of saying that numbers don't tell the full story. Government influence can occur through many channels.

To take just one example, a state company can be organized through a complex chain of interlocking holding companies. The publicly listed company may simply be the visible part of a deeper network. "The holding company may hide behind the layers of ownership and avoid governance reform. This hierarchical ownership structure creates degrees of distance between the holding company and its overseas subsidiaries" (Milhaupt 2015).

The hierarchy of state control can be confusing to outsiders. How to peel the onion of the Chinese corporate system?

China's Own Classification

A good way to begin is to take a look at the taxonomy the country itself uses. China officially distinguishes between firms classified as state controlled by Beijing or state controlled by local governments. There are 117,000 state firms in China with assets of 85 trillion renminbi. Beijing controls 106, while the remaining 116,000 are owned by provincial governments. In 2003, following China's entry into the World Trade Organization (WTO), China carved out a special agency responsible for the country's wholly owned state firms. With the cumbersome name of the State-Owned Assets Supervision and Administration Commission, SASAC was put in charge of these unwieldy yet powerful giants. These included the giant firms controlling oil, telecommunications, aerospace, power, coal, and other key sectors of the economy.

There are actually three layers of SASAC control. Apart from the top SOEs in key industries, and the local enterprises, there is another group of smaller SOEs in sensitive areas such as culture and media.

Apart from direct ownership by central or local governments, Beijing also has a role in their management. This is particularly true of the top 106 firms directly under the ownership of the central government in Beijing. To cite one example of this control, at one point the leadership was debating reshuffling the chief executive of one of the state-owned banks. One of the country's most senior leaders in the ruling State Council called the CEO and asked him point-blank: Would he like to take over the CEO role at one of the other state banks? He declined, saying that he would prefer to continue making progress at his current institution, where he had built years of experience and connections. With that one phone call the management decision was made (OCR 2010).

The power of Beijing becomes more fluid as one moves further down the hierarchy. Provincial state firms have a myriad of competing claims on their operations. Foremost is party control; all firms have to have a senior party leader who may wield more control than the actual CEO. But apart from party control, within each province there are a variety of governmental agencies all with their tentacles in the flesh of state corporates. These include the local branches of the regulators, which for banks would include the China Banking Regulatory Commission (CBRC) and the People's Bank of China (PBOC), the Ministry of Commerce, and the National Development and Reform Commission (NDRC). Local governments, too, have their hands in the pot, as the state firms are usually big employers of local workers, often borrow money from local banks, and may generate profits that can be taxed or otherwise utilized by local governments.

This is all made more complicated by a plan to merge the state giants into larger conglomerates by 2020. The plan was approved in 2015 with a focus on energy, resources, transportation, and telecommunications (Wei 2015).

This makes for a much more complex—and confusing—group of actors in the system than most Westerners imagine. However, in order to understand China's global ambitions on the world corporate stage, it is important to analyze the flow of power between all these competing groups.

A Guide to State Control

One of the most subtle descriptions of state control in China was assembled by Curtis Milhaupt and Li-Wen Lin of Columbia University. Instead of utilizing the typical classification of firms by ownership, the authors capture the opaque world in which Chinese corporations operate using a more subtle methodology. Although they are law school professors, they eschew typical ownership analysis to draw, instead, on sociological theories of networks and institutions. They refer to a "networked hierarchy" of control. As they note:

> Networked hierarchy is our term for the way top-down governance features within individual state-controlled corporate groups are coupled with extensive linkages to other state-controlled institutions. Institutional bridging is our term for the pervasive use of personnel-rotation systems, linked equity-ownership structures, and strategic forms of cooperation, such as joint ventures, which serves to unite separate components of the state sector. **These mechanisms create networks among businesses and other organs of the party-state, promote information flow, and provide high-powered incentives to actors in the system by linking corporate performance and political advancement**. (Milhaupt 2013, p. 702; emphasis mine)

When Westerners try to pin down state control in Chinese firms, they miss the fact that this classification may be misleading. Some state firms, like ChemChina, may be state owned but act without much guidance from the state; that's why I refer to the company's chairman as a "bureaucratic entrepreneur." Other corporates may be privately held but are doing the bidding of the state. However, even Milhaupt acknowledges that the nature of control of the firm in China is hard to define with any precision. Milhaupt cites a number of examples of these indeterminate control mechanisms. These include both the Communist Party appointment of senior executives, and the veto power wielded by SASAC over both executive pay, board of directors, and downstream acquisitions.

The chart below provides one example. The authors collected data on the appointment and removal of the top manager of SOEs. Obviously, if you can appoint or remove the top manager, you exercise a great deal of control over the operation of the firm. They discovered that, indeed, SASAC has a great deal of authority over state firms. Over a period of seven years, SASAC removed from one-third to three-quarters of the leaders of national SOEs (Fig. 4.1).

But as I have noted in the case of Syngenta and ChemChina, these controls are quite fluid; in some cases, the state exercises direct control over corporate transactions (e.g., saying no to a merger), and in others, the state can *influence but not directly control* the outcome. In ChemChina/Syngenta, for example, the transaction was put in the state plan as part of the global growth of China's high-tech industries, a clear "yes" vote from the leadership. However, the state-owned banks refused to participate in the transaction, a clear "no" vote from at least one arm of the state—the banks. Ren Jianxin, in his role as dealmaker, had to negotiate between these different poles of state control. Many investors I spoke to when this transaction was still in flux asked why Beijing didn't just order the banks to supply the bank loans to close the deal. What they didn't understand is that all firms operate in the gray area between state and private operations. Beijing often encourages competition between different state actors.

Postal Bank's Private Ambition

To explore this gray area further, with ChemChina/Syngenta, there were examples of involvement by the state that were not formalized. ChemChina had been struggling to raise the financing for the Syngenta acquisition and replace the funds promised by HSBC and Citic. Recall that the main state banks refused to become involved. However, ChemChina company was able to lean on another state bank: The Postal Savings Bank. The Postal Bank agreed to establish a $5 billion fund to support the Syngenta bid (Reuters December 1, 2016).

It was never explained exactly why the Postal Savings Bank was more eager than the other state banks to jump to ChemChina's rescue. However, the form of their support provides a clue to their motivation. First, the bank had just gone public and was eager to make its mark in international finance. Second, it was launching an investment bank separately from the commercial lending institution, and this transaction was seen as the linchpin of its launch. The bank's reputation would be enhanced domestically and in Europe. Moreover, the Postal Savings Bank planned to offload the

Appointments and Removals of Leaders of the Chinese Central Enterprises[124]

Year	Number of Central Enterprises	Number of Central Enterprises with Appointments or Removals	Percentage of Central Enterprises with Appointments or Removals	Number of Appoint-ments	Number of Removals
2003	196	65	33.16%	150	79
2004	178	77	43.26%	224	155
2005	169	113	66.86%	237	158
2006	159	101	63.52%	323	136
2007	155	90	58.06%	317	113
2008	148	95	64.19%	358	146
2009	129	97	75.19%	312	145

Leaders include members of boards of directors, CEOs, Vice-CEOs, chief accountants, secretaries of the Party Committee, deputy secretaries of the Party Committee, and secretaries of the Party's Discipline Inspection Committee.

Fig. 4.1 Turnover Among State Firm CEOs. Source: Ibid., p. 740

debt to private individuals through the securitization and sale of Wealth Management Products, reducing its own risk. Its weakness as a competitor to other state banks was precisely what led it to support ChemChina. So, the Postal Savings Bank was following its own financial guidelines even though it is owned by the government.

Networked SOEs

Li-Wen Lin of the University of British Columbia calls these behind-the-scene connections between state firms a "network anatomy." As she explains, "Chinese SOEs are embedded in a network composed of dense and complex links with the state. Shareholding ties, albeit important, are only one of the many relations with the state" (Li-Wen Lin 2017a). Most of these connections exist *outside of any legal structure* and thus are almost impossible (or at least very difficult) for outsiders to analyze.

There are many non-legal structures, according to Li-Wen Lin. Most important are business groups where state firms collaborate with each other outside of any formal structure. These groups share financing through separately owned banks, along with information distributed through research institutes.

From the government, control extends beyond SASAC to include the Party's Organization Department, the Ministry of Human Relations and Security, and the Ministry of Finance (Ibid., p. 5). As an example of this "soft" institutional control, every year 50 or 60 central SOE managers are seconded to SASAC for one year, while SASAC managers then move down to the central SOEs. This encourages linkages that help to ensure that state firms act in accordance with state policies (Ibid., p. 6). Untangling this complex machinery is not easy.

Government and Influence

We've looked at structures of power. But what about actual behavior? For the purposes of this book, I have focused on specific transactions to track the flow of funds as an indication of where power lies. More theoretically, how much are Chinese corporates doing the bidding of the state as opposed to merely maximizing their profits in a capitalist manner?

One study by economists for the US Federal Reserve drew some conclusions about the different incentives between state and non-state firms. First, they noted a significant distinction between SOE and private firms when it comes to use and access to capital. Firms are highly sensitive to their rate of profits (measured by internal cash flows) and cost of capital, from bank loans and trade credit. Not surprisingly, government-owned firms tend to be less concerned with their level of profitability and also tend to have better access to bank loans (Cull 2015).

An Informal Taxonomy of State Control

As I have been indicating in the discussion on China's political structure, the ways the state can influence foreign investments and corporate control more generally can be quite subtle. The laws of China describe certain formal relationships with economic activity, but often less formal structures that aren't captured by the laws are more important.

Political Scientist William Norton refers to a concept called "economic statecraft" to delineate the relationship between a country's international relations and its internal economy. He outlines five key elements: (1) Compatibility of goals between the state and the commercial actors that carry on the economic activity of the state, (2) commercial market structure, (3) unity of the state, (4) the reporting relationship between the commercial firm and the state, and (5) relative distribution of resources between the state and commercial actors (Norris 2016). I am here focusing primarily on the relationship between the state and commercial actors. However, as we have noted earlier, these distinctions could apply to many firms that act within the Chinese political system.

The China Dealmaking Hierarchy

To that end, I have devised my own back-of-the envelope hierarchy of how power flows through the system to direct foreign investment. For recipients of Chinese investment, understanding this type of hierarchy is important when forming policy.

The categories below are broad, but I believe they can help foreigners slice into the complex web of power in China. I break this power flow into three categories: Direct ownership, political control, and access to capital. Each of these categories has its own dynamic and internal catalysts.

Direct ownership could be ownership through SASAC, equity stakes owned by state entities, or investments by state entities such as China Development Bank (CDB) or China Investment Corp (CIC). As we saw with the telephone call with the CEO of a state bank, asking whether he wished to change jobs, ownership has a direct role in structuring behavior.

Political control covers a broad range of options including formalized regulations that dictate where investments can be made; broad guidelines from the government that set the parameters of external investment; and political influence through non-transparent means such as party control or even informal conversations from influential state actors to corporates. There is much wriggle room for companies acting under this umbrella.

Access to capital refers to the channels and regulations that govern the methods by which corporates obtain funding. These funding channels include equity and bond raises, bank loans from state (and private) banks, permission to use China's increasingly scarce foreign exchange, shadow banking loans, and more general rules governing the capital available for mergers and acquisitions.

A Taxonomy of State Control over Corporates in China

- Direct Ownership
  - SASAC
  - Equity stakes owned by state entities
  - Investments by state entities such as CDB or CIC.

- Political Control
  - Formalized regulations that dictate where investments can be made
  - Broad guidelines from the government that set the parameters of external investment
  - Political influence through non-transparent means such as party control or even informal conversations from influential political actors
- Access to Capital
  - SOE bank loans
  - Private bank loans
  - Foreign exchange
  - Shadow loans
  - Merger rules
  - Foreign exchange

We admit this is an informal taxonomy of corporate control in China. But this taxonomy is a useful guide for foreign governments, bankers, and corporations to use when analyzing the power structures that govern offshore Chinese investments. What are some examples of the above classifications?

Direct Ownership

China's policy banks, which include the CDB and Export-Import Bank, have a direct influence on China's corporate growth through direct investments and loans in foreign firms. These banks loaned $100 billion outside of China in just 2016, a significant contribution to China's total $170 billion in foreign investment (Dollar 2017a). The policy banks originally invested directly in overseas firms. CIC was set up in 2007 to invest China's wealth globally. It now has $800 billion in assets including $200 billion overseas (Zhu 2017b) (Fig. 4.2).

However, CIC also was a direct investor in foreign companies. CIC suffered losses when it invested in foreign banks and other institutions following the US financial crisis, including Morgan Stanley. A report by China's national auditor found CIC made 12 overseas investments between 2008 and 2012 that incurred losses or potential losses because of "dereliction of duty, inadequate due diligence, a lack of post-investment

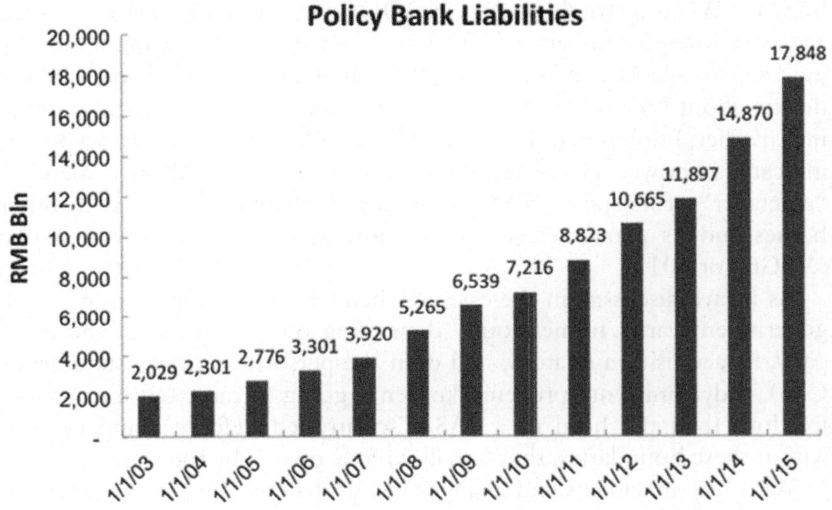

Fig. 4.2 Liabilities Among China's Policy Banks

management and other problems" (Anderlini 2014a). In 2015, CDB provided capital to fund China State Shipbuilding's offer for cruise ship company Carnival Corporation.

Many of the investments by the policy banks have been directed into commodities and resource companies. In part, this has reflected China's strategic drive to control its source of raw materials. But it also may have been in response to the visible losses in public equity stakes in commercial institutions. The gains and losses of these stakes were visible in their share prices, which was a huge embarrassment to the leadership when some of these holdings collapsed in value following the financial crisis. A private stake in a commodity or private commodity firm is not so easy to publicly value and thus much less visible. Who is going to force the banks to write down a private equity investment when the underlying value would be difficult to ascertain? It's a politically safer investment than in a public company.

SASAC's Role

As I have noted earlier, the biggest owner of Chinese corporates is SASAC, which directly owns 102 Chinese companies. This number does not include approximately 130,000 firms owned by the provincial arms of

SASAC. When Petrochina or CNOOC, the country's two oil giants, acquire a foreign company or invest in resources, it is operating under the guidance of SASAC, and indirectly, the State Council itself. There is much debate about how much control SASAC really wields over these companies. Earlier, I noted that the ability to hire and fire SOE leaders is a potent indicator of power. However, others have argued that SASAC is merely a "caretaker" of its stakes in SOEs, because it shares oversight with other bodies and its personnel control is more symbolic than anything else (McGregor 2012).

As I have discussed in the case of ChemChina, the supervision by the government varies tremendously depending on the nature of the company, its acquisition strategy, and even the personality of the state firm's CEO. A dynamic entrepreneur like Ren is going to carve out much more freedom than the head of a SASAC-controlled defense company. But within these boundaries, they are all directly owned by the state.

With recent reforms and changes in the structure of the government, SASAC has transferred some of its SOE shares to other institutions, primarily China's state-owned Asset Management Companies (AMCs). SASAC's stake declined from 67.3 percent to 23.5 percent, but the AMCs' stakes rose by approximately the same amount. "Just as the state banks moved bad loans off their books into AMCs that they owned, state offices shifted their ownership shares into AMCs that they also owned." This has diluted SASAC's power (Wang 2011, p. 258).

Bank loans from state-owned banks are also highly influenced by politically driven policy decisions. (This is not direct ownership but is related.) China's SOE commercial banks are globally aggressive. Take the BOC, the most internationally established among the big four SOE banks. From 2014 to 2016, the bank's overseas assets rose nearly 50 percent, exceeding the bank's overall growth of 30 percent. Overseas loans rose from 19 percent to 23 percent of the total. Currently, 62 percent of the clients at the bank's overseas institutions are locally based (Xuexing 2017). Overall, SOE foreign bank loans more than tripled from 43 billion renminbi in 2014 to 131 billion renminbi at the end of 2016 (Fig. 4.3).

Although the state banks argue that they lend according to market principles, they cannot go against the wishes of the state (particularly the CBRC and the PBOC). But they benefit by their state connections. During the US financial crisis, many of the Chinese banks were worried about their offshore holdings of foreign exchange in the American banks. There was concern that there could be a bank run that would cause a bank

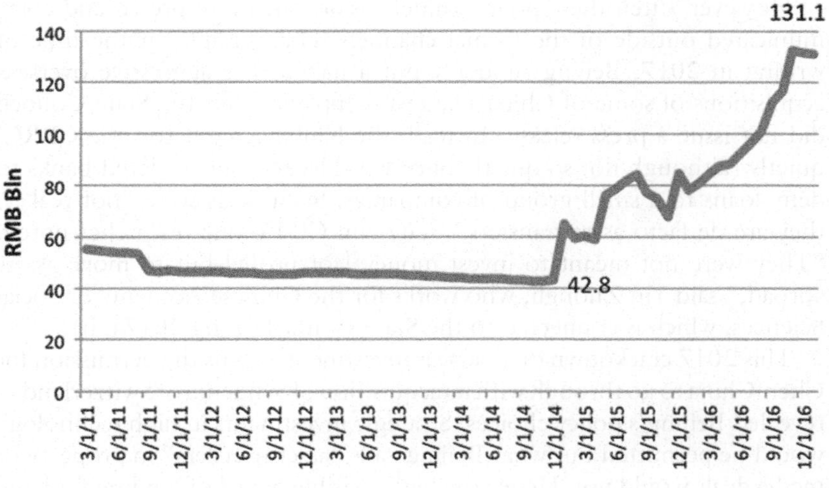

Fig. 4.3 SOE Overseas Loans

collapse. So many put their dollar holdings into the one Chinese bank with access to the Federal Reserve—the BOC. As a result, instead of offering a return to investors, the New York branch of the BOC *started to charge* banks to hold their money. This was a boon to their 2008 profits (Orient Capital Research, Sept. 12, 2016). So there are advantages and disadvantages to being owned by the state.

Political Control

Political control runs the gamut from formal rules to indirect influence over capital flows. Formally, at the top level there are guidelines to overseas investments sanctioned by the State Council. In 2014, China's official news service, Xinhua, issued a statement about the country's international investment strategy. It said China Beijing would increase financial support for Chinese companies going overseas. "The move will raise the international competitiveness of Chinese products, especially equipment products, boost structural upgrading of foreign trade and push manufacturing and financial sectors to a medium-high level," the statement said (Tiezzi 2014). This vague statement provided little clarity to China's intentions.

However, often these policy guidelines are then interpreted and communicated outside of the formal channels. For example, at the time of writing in 2017, Beijing suddenly put a halt to the aggressive overseas acquisitions of some of China's largest companies. But the State Council did not issue a press release. Instead, the banking regulator, the CBRC, quietly (although not so quietly once word leaked out) ordered banks to deny loans to a small group of companies. Such deals were "not real … they are de facto asset transfers," state-run CCTV one researcher noted. "They were not meant to invest money [for profit] but to move assets abroad," said Yin Zhongli, who works for the Chinese Academy of Social Sciences, which is connected to the State Council (Tang 2017a, b).

This 2017 crackdown on overseas investments—plus the permission for ChemChina to go through with its acquisition of Syngenta of Switzerland—revealed Beijing's policy choices. Strategic investments in high technology would be permitted but what Beijing calls "asset transfers" in property or media deals would not. Hence the highly visible denial of funding for large Chinese corporates including Dalian Wanda, HNA, and Anbang. These policy statements (often not openly communicated) are a powerful indication of the current thinking within the top leadership. But they also show how scattershot and ad hoc policymaking is in China; it's too difficult for all factions to agree on a course of action and issue a formal statement. Instead, it's much easier to just quietly change course behind the scenes through an institution like the CBRC.

Access to Capital

This is always the most interesting route of control as it can be completely opaque to outsiders. The above example of using the CBRC instead of a legal route to deny outbound acquisitions is the one that became known only because it was obviously leaked. But these decisions on strategic priorities are made constantly at lower levels of the financial hierarchy. The complex mix of funding for the Syngenta transaction, described earlier, is one example. There was no clear policy so the banks all had to jockey for position between themselves.

As the restrictions on funding for Wanda's overseas transaction indicated, political edicts can be formalized through direct regulatory action or through "back-channels" through the funding routes.

However, these two forms of power—political and financial—can act at cross-purposes. One example occurred in 2016 in the property sector in China. There were public announcements and less public regulations designed to reduce mortgage lending in order to slow the rising rate of property prices. *Bloomberg News* reported one set of regulatory demands aimed at the banks:

> Some lenders in those cities have been asked to suspend distributing new home loans, said the people, who asked not to be named as the change hasn't been made public. Central bank branches in the cities communicated verbally with lenders within their jurisdictions, said the people, who didn't identify the affected cities or say how long the mortgage limits will last. Banks in Shanghai were told not to increase mortgage lending from the previous month, another person with knowledge of the matter said. The central bank didn't respond to questions sent Monday via fax. (Bloomberg News, November 29, 2016)

However, that same year, the CBRC quietly instructed banks to remove mortgages from their overall quota for property-related lending, which had included both developer and mortgage loans (Orient Capital Research, May 23, 2016). This was the exact opposite of the restraints on mortgage lending. Beijing wanted to have its cake and eat it too, that is, to continue supplying credit to the property industry to maintain GDP growth and inflated land sales that contributed to local tax revenue, while simultaneously restraining consumer demand. Although it did not affect company overseas sources of capital, indirectly, this flow of credit provided developers with additional funds they could use for foreign expansion.

One of the most critical tools in Beijing's toolbox is its control of foreign exchange. The State Administration of Foreign Exchange (SAFE), which is under the PBOC, is responsible for doling out foreign currency to companies seeking to acquire assets abroad. We've already discussed the political problems faced by ChemChina in its bid for Syngenta and also some of the ways that SAFE has altered its criterion for administering foreign exchange. Even SAFE, though, has to negotiate with banks and corporations when it makes these crucial decisions about who to permit the use of foreign exchange.

I would not argue that this taxonomy is the final word in analyzing China's overseas investment push. However, I see it as a useful shorthand tool. Sometimes a spade, although smaller, is quicker than a shovel.

Bibliography

Anderlini, Jamil. 2014a. Chinese Fund CIC Under Fire Over Overseas Losses. *Financial Times*, June 18, London.

Anderlini, James 2014b. Chinese Fund CIC Under Fire Over Overseas Losses. *Financial Times*, June 18, Beijing.

Dollar, David. 2017a. *Yes, China Is Investing Globally—But Not So Much in Its Belt and Road Initiative*. Washington, DC: Brookings Institution. May 8.

———. 2017b. *China's New Investment Rules*. Washington, DC: Brookings Institution. August 23.

Giorno, Guy. 2012. *Investment Canada Act: State-Owned Enterprise Policy*. Toronto: Fasken Martineau Institute. December 19.

Lardy, Nicholas. 2014. *Markets Over Mao*. Washington, DC: Peterson Institute.

Lin, Li-Wen. 2017a. National Champions: Governance Change Through Globalization? *University of Pennsylvania Asian Law Review* 11 (1), Article 3.

Lin, Wen-li. 2017b. *A Network Anatomy of Chinese State-Owned Enterprises*. San Domenico di Fiesole: European University Institute, Robert Schuman Centre for Advanced Studies. July.

McGregor, James. 2012. *No Ancient Wisdom, No Followers*. Connecticut: Prospecta Press.

Milhaupt, Curtis J. 2013. We Are the (National) Champions: Understanding the Mechanisms of State Capitalism in China. *Stanford Law Review*, 65: 697–760.

Milhaupt, Curtis J., and Wentong Zheng. 2015. Beyond Ownership: State Capitalism and the Chinese Firm. *Georgetown Law Journal* 103: 665–722.

Norris, William J. 2016. *Chinese Economic Statecraft: Commercial Actors, Grand Strategy, and State Control*. Ithaca: Cornell University Press.

Orient Capital Research. 2010. Interview.

Tang, Frank. 2017a. China Takes Harsher Tone Against Big Dealmakers, Alleging 'Asset Transfer'. *South China Morning Post*, July 19, Hong Kong.

———. 2017b. China Takes Harsher Tone Against Big Dealmakers, Alleging 'Asset Transfer'. *South China Morning Post*, July 17, Hong Kong.

Tiezzi, Shannon. 2014. China Urges Companies to 'Go Global'. *The Diplomat*, December 25, Washington, DC.

Wei, Lingling. 2015. China Economic Plan Calls for Mergers, Public Listings By 2020. *Wall Street Journal*, September 7, Beijing.

Xuexing, Jiang. 2017. BOC's Overseas Lending Outgrows Domestic Loans. *China Daily*, March 23, Beijing.

Zhu, Levin. 2017a. *Zhu Rongji's Son: China Has Overbuilt Houses for 300 Million People*. Shanghai: Chinascope. July 12.

Zhu, Julia. 2017b. China Sovereign Wealth Fund CIC Plans More U.S. Investments: Chairman. *Reuters*, January 16, Hong Kong.

CHAPTER 5

China's Global Tentacles

Abstract We look at the global reach of the Chinese government, economy, and corporations, both state and private. We connect overseas transactions with the difficulty China is facing with outbound capital flows and how it impacts international transactions. One of the key questions is China's use of bank loans to fund corporate purchases and the impact this has on other nations' short of capital. Within the global framework and China's acquisitions, we examine the case of One Belt One Road and its relationship with the themes of state policy and Chinese expansionism. Also examined is the question of China's security interests and its relationship with the country's international corporate takeovers.

Keywords Chinese Academy of Social Sciences • China Railway Engineering • Liabilities • McKinsey • Policy Banks • Brookings Institution • Pirelli

The Currency Problem

China was bleeding money. Not the type of cash you can put into a fireplace and burn, but the kind of money that's even more important: Foreign exchange. In just ten months, from January 2016 until October, the country's foreign exchange reserves fell from \$3.31 trillion to \$3.12

A. Collier, *China Buys the World*,
https://doi.org/10.1007/978-981-10-7494-3_5

trillion, *190 billion dollars in less than a year.* And this was down from $3.81 trillion at the beginning of 2015. What was happening?

Unlike most Western countries, where the domestic currency can be freely bought and sold, China has what is called a closed capital account. That means that all transactions have to be approved by the Chinese government before any foreign firm can get its hands on the renminbi or any Chinese citizen or company can obtain foreign currency. Regulating the inflow and outflow of capital has been the bedrock of China's financial system since Deng Xiaoping's economic reforms in the 1980s. The goal has been to keep China's capital locked in the state banks.

There were two reasons for this. First, this allowed the government—through the banks—to allocate funds to whatever economic growth policies were decided in Beijing. And second, through a complicated system of controls, Beijing could collect consumer savings into the banks at low interest rates and then channel these funds into state companies, giving them a cheap source of capital for state investment goals. This policy dance is known as "financial repression"—the average citizen is "repressed" because the state does not provide financial alternatives. In order to control the capital in the banks, the country cannot allow money to leak out of the country. Hence capital controls.

Gradual capital account liberalization started in 1994. Since then, China has removed many restrictions on inbound foreign direct investment and loosened controls over portfolio investments. Beijing has been perfectly happy to allow foreigners to bring money into the country. However, outbound investments, and financial flows in both directions, have generally been strictly limited.

Some economists believe a closed capital account is a benefit for emerging markets. Olivier Jeanne, Arvind Subramanian, and John Williamson of the Peterson Institute for International Economics conducted a comprehensive survey of the literature on capital account liberalization and economic growth and found that there is no clear-cut relationship between the two. Indeed, the authors (two of them former IMF officials) go so far as to conclude that "the international community should not seek to promote totally free trade in assets—even over the long run—because free capital mobility seems to have little benefit in terms of long run growth." Columbia University economists José Antonio Ocampo, Shari Spiegel, and Joseph Stiglitz as well as Harvard University economists Kenneth Rogoff and Carmen Reinhart have also shown that capital account liberalization is associated with an increased incidence of banking crises in a country (Gallagher 2014).

Chinese policymakers are always willing to point out the dangers of an open capital account. They point to the 1997 Asian Financial Crisis, when a spate of excessive lending blew up Thailand and other countries, leading to a massive withdrawal of capital controlled by global investment funds.

But there's a downside to a closed capital account, a kind of a devil's pact. It is formally known as the Impossible Trinity. A country cannot have a fixed foreign exchange rate, free capital movement, and an independent monetary policy. Something has to give. China has chosen to control its exchange rate and its monetary policy, and be damned about free-flowing capital.

None of this mattered very much when China was recording double-digit GDP growth, and domestic investors and state actors were happy to park their money in the world's fastest growing economy. Why would anyone want to invest anywhere else when they lived in a country growing at more than 10 percent a year? However, things changed markedly when the economy slowed, an anti-corruption campaign became a formal policy under Xi Jinping, and debt skyrocketed. All of a sudden, Chinese were dying to get their money out of China. Things were starting to look too risky internally.

The PBOC Faces a "Quandary"

The slowing economy put officials in charge of controlling the economy in a quandary. Some blamed overseas speculators for the problem. Zhou Xiaochuan, the powerful and intellectually well-trained head of the central bank, cited speculators as the problem. "As uncertainties have recently been abounded in the global financial market, some speculative forces are targeting China. Under normal circumstances, China is not the target of international speculators because it is not easy to make money due to the sheer size of the economy and abundant resources. As a matter of fact, China experienced mainly capital inflows for many years, some of which might be hot money. It is nothing strange that such money withdraws from China when opportunities are good" (Zhou 2016). However, there were many other forces at work. And one of them was overseas acquisitions.

All of a sudden, in November 2016, Beijing began targeting overseas investments. Once glorified as a sign of China's growing international influence, these foreign deals were now seen as giant money laundering machines for Chinese corporations.

The numbers certainly looked staggering. By the first half of 2016, Chinese companies' offshore investments had quadrupled to $134 billion in 493 transactions from $32.7 billion in 123 transactions two years earlier. ChemChina's US$43 billion bid for Syngenta was the biggest ever by a Chinese buyer, but even after deducting this megadeal, outbound M&A grew by 161 percent with 24 deals larger than US$1 billion. Consulting firm PWC analyzed the flows and came up with four reasons for the jump in transactions:

1. Seeking advanced technologies, know-how, and brands to bring back to China
2. Looking to overseas markets as a source of inorganic growth, taking advantage of available and competitive financing
3. Leveraging multiple arbitrage
4. Hedging against a declining Yuan (Brown 2016)

From the point of view of the People's Bank of China (PBOC), the question was how much did the value of the yuan matter to this flood of deals. The country's foreign exchange reserves plunged $45.7 billion in October 2016 from September to $3.12 trillion. The Institute of International Finance based in Washington estimated that net outflows doubled to $207 billion in the third quarter of 2016 from the previous three months. China was bleeding money and these mergers were beginning to look like one important reason.

Beijing Cracks Down on Capital Flight

Suddenly rumors of a clampdown on transactions sprouted like dandelions after a spring rain. On November 26, 2016, the *Wall Street Journal* reported a new set of restrictions on offshore mergers. Targeted for particular scrutiny by the pending measure were "extra-large" foreign acquisitions valued at $10 billion or more per deal, property investments by state-owned firms above $1 billion, and investments of $1 billion or more by any Chinese company in an overseas entity unrelated to the investor's core business (Wei 2016).

Internal discussions began to leak that suggested the beginning of darker examinations where the authorities would screen all outbound transactions. In a meeting held on November 30, 2016, the State Council would begin requiring "stepped-up supervision" of state assets deployed overseas. The meeting called for "stronger supervision of overseas state assets, to gradually realize regular scrutiny and inspection of [state-owned] enterprises' financing and investment overseas, change of property rights and fund management, to ensure the safe operation of overseas assets and to increase the value of assets" (Wu 2016).

Despite the harsh-sounding rhetoric, the new crackdown raised some thorny issues. First, how would the bureaucracy handle all these examinations? They were being swamped with huge, multimillion-dollar transactions at the rate of one or two per day. Western analysts like to think of China as a giant, efficient political machine—but often it is nothing more than a scattered group of harried bureaucrats trying to make an unworkable system function. As an example, in 2015 I had lunch with two senior bankers at a large state bank based in Beijing. They were in charge of international transactions. I asked them, how do you vet any requests for foreign exchange. "We can't," the bank's deputy general manager told me. "We ask the company for paperwork and often they will just tell us no. Since they're state-owned, we can't push them." At one point in 2016, State Administration of Foreign Exchange (SAFE), a unit of the PBOC responsible for the country's currency, was charged with approving any offshore merger above $10 million. Bankers told me that was nearly impossible given the number of deals and the lack of trained personnel to handle them.

Starting in late 2015, Chinese corporates discovered that exports could be gamed, particularly those in China's own territory of Hong Kong. In 2016, imports from Hong Kong experienced stunning accelerated growth even while total imports declined for 17 consecutive months. According to the General Administration of Customs, imports from Hong Kong increased 242.6 percent YoY to US$2.4 billion in May, which for the year until then added US$8.33 billion, representing an annual growth rate of 146.8 percent.

According to an experienced customs clearing agent, "Growth momentum like this was very unusual given the overall grim picture of imports and exports, though the base was comparatively small in 2015. The number was likely inflated by bogus transactions that served for capital flight. It's a common practice among importers," said an industry analyst. In addition, more than half of imported goods from Hong Kong are jewelry, precious metals, and related products. "These low-weight but high-value commodities are ideal for virtual-high price quotations."

Although a spokesperson for the Ministry of Commerce at the time attributed the exceptional values to seasonal factors such as Spring Festival in February, imports from Hong Kong subsequently for another three months in a row at greater magnitude. "Hong Kong, the closet free port to mainland China, has long been used as a transfer stop for capital outflow. It's a cradle of inflated import and export prices, false invoices and shipping documents," according to a trading agent who specialized in imports and exports between Hong Kong and mainland China. Could the same type of games be going on with corporate mergers?

To distinguish capital flight from normal capital outflow, rather than only focusing on the scale of outbound M&A, I asked two questions:

1. Where was the money invested?
2. In general, does the capital flow back?

By industry, in 2014, 83.7 percent of China's stock of Overseas Direct Investment (ODI) was accounted for in leasing and the commercial services industry (US$322.4 billion by the end of 2014, 36.5 percent, primarily in investment holdings), the financial industry (US$137.6 billion, 15.6 percent), the mining industry (US$123.7 billion, 14 percent), the wholesale and retail industry (US$103.0 billion, 11.7 percent), and the manufacturing industry (US$52.4 billion, 5.9 percent) totaling US$739.1 billion. However, much lower-than-expected profitability of these overseas projects is what truly defines the nature of China's ODI largely as capital flight. According to a survey conducted by the Chinese Academy of Social Sciences, over half of Chinese companies are making a profit on their overseas projects, 24 percent of them are breaking even, and the remaining 24 percent are making a loss. Nevertheless, the survey results were considered to be false, according to one of our interviewees, who works at the Foreign Trade Arbitration Commission. "If you ask me, over 90 percent of overseas investments make a loss. Money is squandered once it is transferred to foreign bank accounts. No one cares how the money is invested or how it is secretly distributed among personal accounts."

Debt as a Weapon

One of accusations thrown at China is that it uses its labor force, corporations, and financial resources to muscle into less developed nations. Often, instead of bringing a new source of investment, the Chinese intervention does more to satisfy China's overcapacity problem among its state firms, and tie the recipient nations' fortunes to China, than help the local country.

Much of this, unfortunately, is true. While the debate about subsidies, and the value of the currency, become quite technical and difficult to unravel, the evidence against China in less well-developed countries is relatively strong. This is particularly true in Africa, but other nations are also targets. One author noted: "Is China only using its vast construction resources to build overseas infrastructure for trade, while keeping its surplus of contractors employed? Or is it establishing a permanent footprint for strategic purposes in the developing world?" (Lelyveld 2017).

In 2015, Sri Lanka borrowed $6 billion from China to pay for Chinese construction of a new port city on land reclaimed from the sea in a project that President Xi boasted would create 83,000 jobs. In 2017, Sri Lanka balked at the size of the loan, eventually agreeing to a deal that would convert $6 billion in loans to an equity stake owned by China. This agreement would give China ownership of a key port on the waterway between Asia and Africa. There was an underlying suspicion that deals like this were specifically designed to overload the local country with debt, forcing that country to hand over ownership to pay for its bank loans. Due to public protests, the actual sale agreed to in July 2017 reduced the stake to 70 percent, down from 80 percent but still giving one of China's larger SOEs, China Merchants Port Holdings, majority control (Mallawarachi 2017).

However, the story is complicated because of the mix of funding that nations utilize for development. The case of Namibia is instructive. There, headlines declaimed that the country had fallen into hock to China to the tune of billions of dollars of debt. No, said Jyhjong Hwang, the Senior Research Assistant at the China-Africa Research Initiative at Johns Hopkins SAIS.

Hwang cites an article, "Is China the World's New Colonial Power?," in May 2017. The article states that "infrastructure is welcome, but as projects made possible by loans—financed by the Chinese—they have saddled the economy with debt." In the end it turns out that only some 12 percent of Namibia's $6.24 billion of external debt was owed to China. The majority of its foreign debt resulted from the sale of sovereign bonds (Hwang 2017).

Another example of China using state funding to control offshore deals occurred in Thailand. China had agreed to provide capital to pay for a high-speed rail link with Thailand. However, negotiations broke down over the financial terms for the 253-kilometer Bangkok-Nakhon Ratchasima route, which will need an estimated $5 billion investment. China reportedly requested the option to "seize the other assets of the Thai government" if Thailand defaulted on debt payments. China argued it was offering the same terms as it did for a rail line in Laos. There, it would be able to take charge of five mines if Laos failed to repay the debt. "We, the Thai government, will not yield to China's demand, because in our history we're a very honest debtor and have never failed to pay back foreign debts. If China insists on this asset guarantee, we will not borrow from China," according to the Thai Minister of Transport Arkhom Termpittayapaisith (Chatrong 2017).

The broader issue is twofold: First, China often boosts its investment totals to convince the world it is a significant investor and should be taken seriously, while in reality it is more cautious. Second, as I have detailed in this book, there are many financial and corporate actors involved in China's overseas transactions, and they all have their own agendas and financial pressures. Attributing malevolent state interests to every transaction without careful scrutiny leads to slipshod analysis and faulty reasoning. However, in some cases—as with the Thai Rail loan—it is clear the Chinese state is pushing its own strategic agenda.

OBOR's Problematic Financing

If ever foreigners could point to a government-run program to put China on the global corporate map, that program would be "One Belt One Road," or OBOR. However, the alternative name coined internally in China is perhaps more illustrative: One Belt One Trap.

OBOR was displayed to the world by Xi in May 2017 in a global forum in Europe attended by 29 heads of state and dozens of ministerial-level national delegations. The ambitious plan would have Chinese state firms invest in 65 nations in a broad swath of the world stretching from China's borders into Europe. OBOR and related projects will invest in countries that represent 55 percent of world Gross National Product (GNP), 70 percent of the global population, and 75 percent of known energy reserves. China has agreed to provide a total of about $100 billion to support OBOR through three new infrastructure funds: $40 billion to the Central Asia-focused Silk Road Fund, $50 billion to a new Asian Infrastructure Investment Bank (AIIB), and $10 billion to a New Development Bank (Godemont 2015).

Domestically, OBOR is designed to boost China's global trade, improve foreign economic relations, and provide new destinations for overcapacity among Chinese companies, particularly those in the huge infrastructure sector, such as steel and concrete. However, OBOR has been perceived abroad as an attack on America's influence in Asia and a testament to the rising power of China globally. Chinese Vice Foreign Minister Zhang Yesui has stated that China's OBOR is "not directed against any specific country or organization" (Ibid.).

However, some Western commentators have seen OBOR as a disguised attack on Western economic and ideological control over the world's economies. As one think tank report noted:

> Global reactions to OBOR and preliminary studies have tended to focus on either its geopolitical implications ("gamers") or its likely developmental consequences. Gamers have speculated about the implications of these plans for China's position in the international system and its role in the system of global governance, including the question of whether new financial institutions such as the AIIB will complement or undermine the Western-led system of development financing and global governance. (Cooley 2016)

But those who are actually making the investments, including companies and banks, are definitely, if not openly, skeptical about the plan. Their concern is twofold. First, political risk for overseas investments generally is quite high for Chinese companies with little experience or knowledge about norms in other countries, a problem even worse in some of the emerging markets OBOR is focused on. And second, finding good projects in these states is a challenge when the banks and corporates have little on-the-ground knowledge of the economic environment. So far, OBOR has *not* been an important factor in the allocation of ODI. A simple calculation illustrating this is that the 68 OBOR countries had received 12 percent of Chinese ODI as of end of 2015; those same countries had received 17 percent of global FDI (2011 data). OBOR is relatively new, so this could change over time. But for 2016, China announced that 8.5 percent of its ODI flow went to OBOR countries (without giving a detailed country breakdown) (Dollar 2017). "Yes, China is investing globally—but not so much in its belt and road initiative" (Washington: Brookings Institution).

The discrepancy between China's stated intention for the region (bringing China in closer partnership with OBOR countries) and the reality is quite striking. *Bloomberg News* noted the following issues—all negative for a positive spin on OBOR:

- The government's Belt and Road plan mentions 18 provinces, of which 13 are less developed. On average, these 13 provinces saw GDP growth slowdown of 4 ppt in the three years since the start of scheme, relative to the three years before. That's compared with a national average slowdown of 1.5 ppt.
- Chinese outbound investment along the route was $14.5 billion in 2016, down 2 percent.

- Chinese firms' construction and engineering contracts in the region in 2016 were $126 billion, up 36 percent from 2015.
- Total trade between China and the OBOR countries fell 3 percent in 2016, compared with a 9 percent rise in 2013.
- China's trade surplus with the region is increasing, up to $250 billion in 2016 from $105 billion in 2013. OBOR countries may begin objecting to this difference.
- The Pew Global Attitudes survey shows the balance of views on China in Belt and Road countries basically unchanged (Orlik 2017).

In Central Asia, Beijing has become the largest source of capital. China provided loans for energy worth $8 billion to Turkmenistan and $13 billion to Kazakhstan. In two other regions, Kyrgyzstan and Tajikistan, where China has financed highway projects, the Export-Import Bank of China is the largest single external creditor, with 49 percent and 36 percent of their respective government debt (Cooley 2016).

One Indian think tank blames many OBOR problems on rampant growth of shadow credit. "Shadow banking and Ponzi schemes are rampant in China and could hurt its economy. Besides, the Chinese market is flooded with uninsured wealth management instruments and zombie companies which, the think tank said, can derail OBOR project" (Chaudhury, May 30, 2017).

Speaking of political risk, between 2005 and 2015, more than $250 billion of foreign investments by Chinese firms failed (AEI Tracker). "For us, the No. 1 consideration is political risk," according to Gordon Li, chairman of China Merchant Group's international business department (Shi 2017). More than three-quarters of Chinese companies in one survey said political risk was the most important risk in overseas investments. These include policy changes, political unrest, and government expropriation (Ibid., Shi).

Yin Yili, vice president at a division of China Communications Construction Co., one of the country's largest state-owned companies, is concerned about the costs of lack of political knowledge. "Over these past years, we've paid a great price and suffered big losses. We've paid a large amount in tuition fees. A lot of times they (Chinese firms) only see a bevy of opportunities, but not pitfalls underfoot," Yin said. "There are more than 200 countries and regions in the world, and not every place is worth investment" (Ibid., Shi).

The Chinese Commerce Ministry revealed that 65 percent of Chinese investments abroad—including Belt and Road projects—had incurred losses. State-funded insurance company Sinosure has provided $2.8 trillion in insurance support to international projects and suffered claims of $9.5 billion (Fun 2017).

My interviews confirmed these problems. The general manager of a state-owned bank in Beijing told us that her department was scrambling for OBOR investments, essentially to get the Beijing leadership off their backs. "We are looking for investments in the OBOR region but don't have the manpower to do proper due diligence," she told me. "Do you know of any investment opportunities there?"

We recently sat down with a young analyst with the National Development and Reform Commission (NDRC) in charge of assessing risks for OBOR. Over coffee in a charming chain in Beijing's trendy San Li Tun bar area, the analyst explained the pressures on bureaucrats, companies, and banks to "chalk one up for the team" with an OBOR investment that would placate Xi and his top Lieutenants in Beijing. But there are others who see it as part of China's rising importance in the world economy.

"Xi is determined to push it forward. Some people in government think it's a good opportunity for China to lead the train for globalization. The U.S. Is cashing out and they don't want to support globalization. A lot of economies are not doing well. This is an opportunity for China to support them," he said.

However, there are concerns that China is squandering its hard-earned capital on overseas projects that would be better spent domestically.

"Some people are concerned that the Chinese economy is not doing well and we don't have that much money to invest abroad. This is a burden to the economy, especially with the reserves dropping. Half think the reserves are too high and more should be spent on foreign investments, while half think they're dropping too fast."

Even within the top levels of the Chinese bureaucracy there is a debate about what OBOR actually is and how much has been invested in it. There are no "official" agreed statistics on OBOR investment. The Ministry of Commerce has a total figure, while the NDRC has a database containing a tally of OBOR investments. This number is confidential—although external estimates run around $200 billion—and may not even be realistic as it includes a number of projects that predated the launch of the OBOR program itself. (This database reportedly was questioned by senior Chinese economist Ma Kai an indication of the disputes at the highest levels of government.) The bulk of these projects are in the energy sector and include projects like a giant Liquid Natural Gas project in Russia. Other major areas are "connectivity" infrastructure projects consisting of highways, railways, and ports linking China to transport centers in Eastern, Central, and Western Europe.

"How we get returns from these projects is risky," the NDRC analyst noted. "China, especially the Ministry of Foreign Affairs, argues that they won't be profitable but there will be better foreign relations for China."

The problem is that these risky projects must be paid for by one of the state entities. Foreign observers fail to realize that there is intense competition for capital within the state sector in China. The funds spent by the state are allocated (or initially spent) by specific firms or banks. They must bear the burden of failure, including demotion if a project goes south. That's why the banks have been exceedingly reluctant to make loans for OBOR projects. These loans are often long in duration—generally decades—putting that liability on the banks' balance sheet for a long period of time.

That's why I would argue that it is naive to point to an investment from China and simply declare that it is "owned by the state." That may be true—but even within state organizations there is foot-dragging, along with restrictions, that would alter the calculation of risk and control. In other words, there is a "hierarchy" of the state that affects the nature of these outward investments. For example, if the US Congress were to question an OBOR investment, in say Kazakhstan, as "state-led," I would propose that it makes a difference whether this was an investment by a Beijing SOE, funded by one of the centrally owned investment banks, or a private investment funded by a state bank like the Bank of China. These two, contrasting investments, display significant differences in ultimate objectives, security impact, and control. The first investment may very well have been conducted according to official mandates by the State Council. The second, however, may generally follow the dictates of "Go West, young corporate" but would be run according to more generally accepted principles of capitalist dictates. Security concerns would be less of a factor in the second example.

Outside of China, many skeptics believe that China's grand plans will run aground due to a lack of capital. The Centre for Asia Africa Policy Research in Hyderabad, India, even published a report entitled, "China's Hard Sell." Their report was ticked off by a downgrade of China's bond ratings from the Moody's agency. "Will the new credit rating put brakes on China plans? Frankly, there are no ready answers…Will they succeed? It depends on how the Chinese marshal their energies to blunt the

Moody's critique and show the Chinese sweeten the deals for the cash strapped low income countries, which have come to see their infrastructure nirvana in OBOR" (Economic Times). "China may hit funds roadblock over OBOR, says Think Tank" (India Times, May 30, 2017).

Security or Money

How much is China's international investment driven by security concerns? How much opposition does China confront overseas due to worries about security?

There's no doubt that Western nations are not happy with a lot of China's deals. In July 2016, the British prime minister stunned China by delaying approval of the Hinkley Point nuclear plant, which would have been the UK's first new nuclear plant in 20 years. Senior military and intelligence officials had warned that handing over ownership in Britain's nuclear power industry to China was a threat to the country's national security (O'Neill 2015). In September that year, the prime minister finally backed down, following diplomatic pressure from China and lobbying by domestic energy groups. But the red flag was raised: European countries were going to monitor China's acquisitions.

There was continuing opposition to China's global expansion in the United States. One American think tank backed by the technology industry argued that China has used a variety of unfair tactics to spread the gospel of its corporate might. Citing export subsidies and support for the renminbi, the author said, "China's distortionary, mercantilist policies rob the world of many of the benefits of free trade. Industries produce better products, see higher levels of innovation, and provide larger benefits to all consumers when they are allowed to locate themselves wherever the free market dictates" (Nager 2016).

Much of the American opposition is housed in a small, quietly named organization with the awkward acronym, CFIUS, or the Committee on Foreign Investment in the US). CFIUS is an inter-agency committee that reviews acquisitions that result in foreign control of an American business "in order to determine the effect of such transactions on the national security of the United States" (CFIUS Website).

Over the past decade, CFIUS has shot down a number of proposed deals, including the 2005 acquisition of Unocal by China's oil giant CNOOC. CFIUS approved the Syngenta deal but blocked Philips' attempt to sell its lighting business to a Chinese consortium in early 2016.

Also, Tsinghua Unigroup withdrew from a $3.8 billion investment in Western Digital after the deal was investigated by CFIUS (Le Corre 2016).

More recently, Congress was seeking to block a *financial* transaction on grounds that it could interfere with security—this was a bit of a stretch. A group of Chinese buyers led by Chongqing Casin Enterprise Group sought to buy the Chicago Stock Exchange for $20 million. Congressional staffers demanded that the deal be halted on national security grounds, causing the SEC to stop the transaction. The Securities and Exchange Commission issued a last-minute freeze that put the $20 million transaction on indefinite hold. "When you take into account the risk of cyber-market manipulation and the gamut of concerns we have with China… you certainly have to be wary of this acquisition," said Rep. Robert Pittenger (R., N.C.) (Wall Street Journal, August 27, 2017).

The political opposition in Europe and the United States to China's cross-border deals will depend on a host of local conditions, including the strength and cohesiveness of the Trump administration, the outcome of Brexit, and the general European reaction to the arrival of Chinese corporates. Our goal in this book is to consider the Chinese attitude and policies toward outbound flows—including the security reaction from foreign countries.

Bureaucratically, outbound transactions are primarily reviewed by the Ministry of Commerce and the NDRC. They rely on a 2004 NDRC regulation, Article 18, which states the following for any project:

1. It shall comply with the laws and regulations and the industrial policies of the state, does not harm the sovereignty, security, and public interests of the state, or violate norms of international laws.
2. It shall comply with the requirements for sustainable social and economic development, be conducive to the development of strategic resources required for developing the national economy, and comply with the requirements of the state for adjusting the industrial structure, help to promote the export of fairly competitive technologies, products, equipment, and labor services, and absorb foreign advanced technologies (Bath 2012).

In addition, in 2006, for domestic considerations, the State-Owned Assets Supervision and Administration Commission (SASAC) identified seven "strategic industries" in which the state would keep control and five "pillar industries" where the state would retain influence. Strategic industries were defined to include defense, electricity generation and distribution, petroleum and petrochemicals, telecommunications, coal, civil aviation, and waterway transport. However, this transparency did not extend to international transactions (Gang 2013).

This does not state any strategic imperative to chase after high technology or military applications. However, China has its own Foreign Investment Security Review System for foreign acquisitions of domestic firms (Bath 2012).

China has gradually consolidated its largest state firms. A look at the consolidation provides a clue to China's strategic goals. We can see from Fig. 5.1 below that the sectors that have grown or remained flat in the 13 years to 2011 are energy, tobacco, and power. Tobacco is a separate case due to the huge revenues to the state from the state monopoly. But the other two are clear strategic priorities. Of course, the defense industry is scattered among different firms so there is no easy way of ascertaining the growth of assets in this sector (Fig. 5.1).

There have also been policies published about specific issues relating to security interests. One of the more famous occurred in 2011 and was designed to ensure access to rare earths, most of which have military applications (Bath 2012). This is perhaps the easiest way to understand China's goals: to examine the transactions themselves.

But the evidence is scarce. The majority of transactions cross boundaries. Is a purchase of a technology company designed to enhance China's cybersecurity or improve China's internet industry? Other countries in the world will continue to struggle with the underlying motives behind many Chinese transactions.

	Number of Firms		Gross Industrial		Total Assets	
	1998	2011	1998	2011	1998	2011
Mining and washing of coal	49.5	11.5	81.9	53.6	92.7	72
Extraction of petroleum and natural gas	81.7	40.2	94.5	92.1	98.9	94.7
Manufacture of food	44.1	4.1	29.7	5.8	41.1	9.9
Manufacture of tobacco	87.2	79.1	98.3	99.3	98.2	99.3
Manufacture of textiles	24	1.2	32.2	2.4	46.2	5
Printing, reproduction of recording media	58	8	37.9	11.5	51.2	18.2
Processing of petroleum, coking and nuclear fuel	28.3	10.9	91	68.6	90.3	58.8
Manufacture of chemical products	32.3	5	50.4	18.7	69.5	29.1
Manufacture of medicines	45.3	7.1	49.6	11.8	60.8	20.3
Manufacture of rubber	21	3.1	34.3	12.1	50.7	16.2
Manufacture of general machinery	29.6	3.2	38.4	12.5	60.7	22.3
Manufacture of special machinery	40.9	5.2	41.2	20.5	63.3	32.2
Manufacture of transport equipment	40.1	7.6	67	44	78.2	53.2
Manufacture of communication equipment	29.8	5.2	37.7	8.3	51	19.6
Production and supply of electric power/heat	85.6	66.4	85.4	93	89.1	90.7
Production and supply of water	92.6	61.4	87.8	69.4	90.3	79.6
Production and supply of gas	84	29.9	71.6	44.4	93.7	54.3

Fig. 5.1 Analysis of Sector Growth. Source: Gang 2013

Bibliography

Bath, Vivienne. 2012. *China Companies and Investment—The Balance Between Domestic and International Concerns*, July. Society of International and Economic Law. Singapore: SIEL Conference.

Brown, David. 2016. *PWC M&A 2016 Midyear Review and Outlook*. Hong Kong: PWC. August 10.

Chatrong, Wichita. 2017. China's Loan Terms Rejected. *The Nation*, August 14, Bangkok.

Cooley, Alexander. 2016. The Political Economy of OBOR. *CSIS*, October. Washington, DC.

Dollar, David. May 8, 2017. Yes, China is investing globally—but not so much in its belt and road initiative. Washington: Brookings Institution.

Fun, Ho Wah. 2017. Asean Belt and Road Risks Under Scrutiny. *The Star Online*, July 30, Kuala Lumpur.

Gallagher, Kevin, Jose Ocampo, Ming Zhang, and Yongding Yu. 2014. *Capital Account Liberalization in China: A Cautionary Tale*. Boston University, Pardee Center for School of Global Studies, Policy Brief, Issue 002, July.

Gang, Fan. 2013. *The Role of State Owned Enterprises in the Chinese Economy*. U.S. China 2022. Hong Kong: China-United States Exchange Foundation.

Godemont, Francoise. 2015. *One Belt One Road: China's Great Leap Outward*. European Council on Foreign Relations. Paris: ECFR.

Hwang, Jyhjong. 2017. *Guest Post: Desert Mirage: Fact-checking China in Namibia*, May 9. Www.Chinaafricarealstory.com

Le Corre, Phillip. 2016. *China's Global Rise. Can the EU and the U.S. Pursue a Coordinated Strategy*. Washington, DC: Brookings Institution.

Lelyveld, Michael. 2017. Chinese Investment Lags in Belt and Road Countries. *Eurasia Review*, August 1, Albany/Oregon.

Mallawarachi, Bharatha. 2017. Sri Lanka, China Sign Long-Delayed $1.5 Billion Port Deal. *Reuters*, July 29, Colombo.

McCauley, Robert, and Tom Orlik. 2017. *One Belt, One Road Topic Primer*. Beijing: Bloomberg.

Nager, Adam. 2016. *Calling Out China's Mercantilism*. Washington, DC: International Economy.

O'Neill, Sean. 2015. Nuclear Deal with China Is a Threat to National Security. *The Times*, October 16, London.

Shi, Ting. 2017. It's Extremely Important Whether the Destination Countries Have Good Relations with China or Not. In *Chinese Companies Wary of Political Risks of Xi's Belt and Road*. Hong Kong: Bloomberg.

Wei, Lingling. 2016. China Issuing Strict Controls on Overseas Investment. *Wall Street Journal*, November 26, Beijing.

Wu, Wendy. 2016. China Moves to Limit State Firms' Investments Overseas to Stem Capital Flight. *South China Morning Post*, December 1, Hong Kong.

Zhou, Xiaochuan. 2016. Interview. *Caixin Magazine*, February 15, Beijing.

CHAPTER 6

The Money Behind the Deals

Abstract How is China funding its international exposure? We analyze the sources of capital for these offshore transactions, including policy banks, state banks, private banks, and shadow banks. We provide a breakdown of the profitability of certain transactions to indicate whether they are successful or not. We discuss HNA and the use of shadow banking to fund its acquisitions. We provide an overview of China's policy banks and their application of capital for overseas purposes.

Low Success Rate

Critics of China's pell-mell chase for overseas assets tend to focus on whether the Chinese firms will adversely affect domestic firms or hurt the host country's national security interests. What is overlooked is whether the country can afford them and what the *financial* benefit is to China. These may sound like simple questions, but they are vitally important when analyzing future trends of China's global corporate expansion. It's easy to accuse China of harboring ambitions to become a "neo-imperialist" country, determined to dominate both resources and industries in Asia, Africa, Europe, and the Americas. But it's far more difficult to estimate how *effective* the country's leadership, state corporate giants, and private firms have been—or will be—in achieving these goals. It's equally difficult to calculate how long the country's economy, and banks, can sustain this hectic pace.

A. Collier, *China Buys the World*,
https://doi.org/10.1007/978-981-10-7494-3_6

There's not a great deal of data on what I am calling "the money behind the deals." The banks do not provide an accurate dissection of the destination of their loans, instead using very general categories. Corporates rarely talk about their financing unless they are forced to by disclosure forms or political pressure. Meanwhile, corporate loans through the shadow market are completely off-balance sheet and usually not traceable. For overseas deals, there is also very little transparency, both in profitability and in financing.

There is also very little information once the transaction is completed. And even here there is some debate. For example, according to a survey conducted by the Chinese Academy of Social Sciences, China's main research institute for the government, over half of Chinese companies are making a profit on their overseas projects, 24 percent of them are breaking even and the remaining 26 percent are unprofitable. Nevertheless, the survey results may be incorrect, according to one of our interviewees at the Foreign Trade Arbitration Commission. "If you ask me, over 90 percent of overseas investments make a loss. Money is squandered once it is transferred to foreign bank accounts. No one cares how the money is invested or how it is secretly distributed among personal accounts" (Orient Capital Research, June 11, 2017).

To attempt to be systematic, I looked at this complex issue of the financial aspects of China's international dealmaking through three metrics:

1. Sources of capital
2. Corporate-wide measures of profitability
3. Analysis of specific transactions

Who's Paying for China's Buying Spree

One method is to look at a subset to understand where the capital is from. For example, let's take the top ten transactions for 2016—totaling $27.6 billion (Fig. 6.1).

Most of these are state firms. To understand the finance behind the deals, I broke out five of the major firms: China State Construction, State Power Investment, Three Gorges, Harbin Electric, and Sinomachine. The results were startling. The firms clearly have been relying heavily on debt to fund their domestic and international expansion. How much is the debt for just these five firms? Net debt at the end of 2016 totaled 734 billion renminbi, or $106 billion. Of course, this debt is supporting a vast

Top Ten Chinese Transactions in 2016	Rmb Bln	
China Railway Engineering	$	3,140
State Construction Engineering	$	2,700
State Power Investment	$	2,640
Three Gorges	$	2,400
China Communications Construction	$	2,300
China Railway Construction	$	2,260
Harbin Electric	$	2,150
China Railway Contruction, China Railway E	$	2,120
Sinomach	$	2,100
State Construction Engineering and China C	$	1,720
China Railway Engineering and AVIC	$	1,500
China Communications Construction	$	1,460
Genertec and Beijing SU Power	$	1,100

Fig. 6.1 Top Ten Chinese Transactions in 2016. Source: Bloomberg

infrastructure of projects, both domestic and foreign, but it gives a taste of how much growth is being supplied by debt.

Another way to look at this is to compare their debt against their equity, which is the value of the assets minus whatever liabilities the firms have. Their combined ratio of debt to equity was quite high—52.3×. Compare that relatively high number with the official rate for foreign investment in China. Under government rules, foreign firms investing into China must contribute anywhere from 40 percent to 70 percent equity compared with debt. This is far lower than the average among the top ten 2016 dealmakers (Lehman). In addition, the average for all companies is 19.2× debt for equity.

Profitability Problems

We also tried to slice the analysis in a different way: by looking at the profitability of these firms. The conclusions were mixed. Their profitability in terms of the use of capital (return on capital) was higher than the median for all firms in China, but their profit margins were lower (Fig. 6.2).

In many cases, Chinese firms are ***buying up***...meaning that they are paying to acquire companies in better shape (higher profitability) than them. On most of these metrics, the acquirers do not come out well.

Another useful analysis is to compare a larger group of Chinese companies making acquisitions (not just the top five or ten) with Chinese firms in general. If we bundle all of the firms that have done outbound

	China State Construction	State Power	Three Gorges	Harbin Electric	Sinomachine	Median	Median in China	Premium/ Discount
Return on Common Equity	17.97	3.6	9.19	1.55	9.08	**9.08**	6.5	1.4
Return on Assets	2.61	0.23	4.27	0.31	1.52	**1.52**		
Return on Capital	8.99	3.78	7.56	0.73	3.44	**3.78**		
Return on Invested Capital	8.43	3.31	5.44	1.03	4.03	**4.03**	3.36	1.2
Margins								
Gross Margin	9.14	21.03	51.3	13.66	5.76	**13.7**	17.16	0.8
EBITDA Margin	7.04	30.87	69.18	2.32	3.08	**7.0**		
Operating Margin	6.32	16.95	47.16	-0.7	2.59	**6.3**	6.67	0.9

Fig. 6.2 Profit ratios for the largest acquiring companies in 2016. Source: Bloomberg

transactions, then we discover that generally the firms making overseas acquisitions are more indebted than Chinese firms in general. These firms had a net debt to equity ratio of 30.2 percent compared with 19.2 percent for all Chinese firms. (The data is for 12 months to July 2017 and would depend to some degree on the year analyzed.)

On other measures, though, these firms don't come out so badly. Their return on equity (ROE)—a measure of their profitability compared with the initial investment—is actually higher than the average Chinese firm. Return on assets (which includes all assets, not just the initial investment) is slightly lower but not by much. Their share price on a price-to-earnings basis is also lower than most firms, which could reflect the contribution of the less profitable state firms in the mix. (This analysis is not weighted by market capitalization.)

One flagrant example of overambitious investing is Citic Group's iron ore purchases in Australia. In September 2017, it was reported that Citic would write down $800 million to $1 billion on its results, its third year of write-downs. Citic spent more than $10 billion constructing the project. The company told the Hong Kong exchange that it expected to take further write-downs in the future (Evans, February 2017).

The company told the Hong Kong exchange it expected to take a further hit to the book value of its flagship iron ore project despite the year's surging iron ore price, given the lower long-term outlook for commodity prices.

One of the more insightful analyses of the success or failure of China's offshore deals comes from former McKinsey China head Gordon Orr and the McKinsey & Co. (Orr 2017). In a report, they came to some interesting conclusions. To wit:

- **High Failure Rate.** Around 60 percent of outbound investments by Chinese companies, close to 300 deals of almost $300 billion, created little or no value for acquirers.
- **Resources Not Winners.** Resources deals often were not successful; 43 percent of the deals done in the past decade (217 deals, representing 56 percent of total outbound investment value) involved natural resources. In 84 percent of the deals they reviewed, representing 89 percent of deal value, these deals did not create value for the acquirer, losing on average 10 percent annually in financial terms.
- **Listed Companies Not Successful.** A second group of transactions with low success rates were investments into listed companies that remained listed post-deal. These accounted for 24 percent of the deals done (119 deals, worth 18 percent of total value). On average, they lost 7 percent of their value per year following the transaction. Majority investments did slightly better, losing only 2 percent per year.
- **Controlling Stake Helps.** For the remaining one-quarter of transactions that did not fall into either the resource or the listed company transactions, 70 percent were successful, as measured by goals including product, technology, or cost issues. The degree of control by the acquiring company did matter. The authors note that 34 percent of the total 505 deals were non-control investments, of which only 30 percent was successful. For the control investments, the success rate rose to 45 percent.
- **Overall Success Rate Low.** Of 505 deals and $432 billion of deal value, only 200, worth $146 billion, were considered successful according to the goals laid out by the corporates (Fig. 6.3).

Sources of Capital: China's Policy Banks

Beijing's Own Bankers

Two banks have been substantial backers of China's overseas expansion: China Development Bank (CDB) and China Investment Corp. (CIC). But they, too, have run into constraints. Both have suffered from experiments in overseas expansion and have had to adjust their strategies.

CDB's mandate "is dedicated to strengthening China's competitiveness and improving people's livelihood." This includes a goal to "facilitate

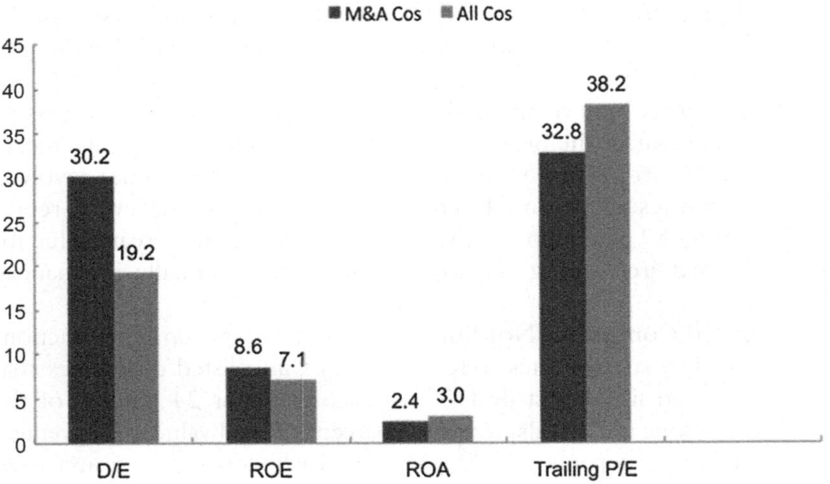

Fig. 6.3 Profitability of Offshore Transactions. Source: Bloomberg

international cooperation and investments, support the implementation of China's "One Belt, One Road," and "Go Global" initiatives" (CDB 2015a). Similarly, CIC "stands ready to join hands with competitive domestic and overseas enterprises to explore and seize quality investment opportunities globally. We will actively explore cross-border investment models that are based on complementarity and win-win cooperation" (CIC 2015b).

CDB has tended to be much more supportive of national state aims—not surprising, given its name.

As one Brookings Institution analyst noted:

> The whole edifice of expansion beyond Chinese borders is connected above all to the role played by the CDB, the largest development bank in the world. Without the CDB, no significant project would ever see the light of day, starting with the enormous infrastructure projects such as the Three Gorges Dam on the Yangtze River. Founded in 1994, the CDB depends directly on central government funding and therefore offers an infallible guarantee, which allows it to set up financing on conditions much better than those offered by its competitors. Since 2007 the threat of seeing its status as a privileged development institution withdrawn has hung over the CDB, on the correct assumption that its position and activities are damaging the viability of all other domestic commercial. (Le Corre 2016)

As a result, CDB poured money into long-term loans to Chinese energy companies operating around the world, from 2005 to 2010 totaling $73.6 billion (Fig. 6.4).

However, a changing attitude toward overseas investments in the late 2000s convinced both banks to shift their focus from commodities and energy to financial institutions. This was guided by an attitude in the leadership that China needed to modernize its domestic financial system. Buying the "expertise" of foreign companies became the new policy.

The strategic focus of CDB is apparent in its proud boast that it supported ChemChina's purchase of the Pirelli Tire Company in Italy. "The Bank led a Chinese syndication of EUR800 million and funded ChemChina's successful acquisition of Pirelli, a leading Italian tire manufacturer, in the largest overseas acquisition transaction in China's manufacturing industry. *This acquisition is expected to help raise the overall competence of the Chinese tire industry to a new level, as it poses to trigger a series of industrial transformations and upgrades*" (CDB Annual Report, p. 45; emphasis mine).

Unfortunately, the banks' aggressive investments occurred just as the West was about to be hit by the tsunami of the mortgage crisis. The

Date	Country	Borrower	Amount ($ billion)	Term (Years)
2005	Russia	Rosneft	6*	6
2008	Venezuela	BANDES	4	3
2009	Russia	Rosneft	15	20
2009	Russia	Transneft	10	20
2009	Brazil	Petrobras	10	10
2009	Venezuela	BANDES	4	3
2009	Turkmenistan	Turkmengaz	4	NA
2010	Venezuela	BANDES	20.6	10
2010	Ecuador	Ministry of Finance	1	4

Fig. 6.4 China Development Bank's energy loans. Source: Brooking's John L. Thornton Center, Erica Downs

declines in the value of investments made by the policy bank—down anywhere from 43 percent to 64 percent—caused them untold grief with the leadership in the State Council (Fig. 6.5).

The National Accounting Office accused CIC of blatant mismanagement. Between 2008 and 2013, CIC made 12 overseas investments that faced losses or potential losses because of "dereliction of duty, inadequate due diligence, a lack of post-investment management and other problems." The *Financial Times* quoted one insider saying the fund's management was a "mess." This was a highly unusual public attack on a state institution (Financial Times, June 18, 2014).

Stung by these failures, in 2015 CIC attempted to carve out its professional money management operations from the separate business of investing in state industries. "CIC's overseas investment businesses are now undertaken by CIC International and CIC Capital, while Central Huijin makes equity investments in key state-owned financial institutions in China as authorized. Independent internal decision-making and management systems were built inside the three subsidiaries to ensure a more clear-cut, professional and targeted division of labor" (CIC Annual Report, p. 4). This is another example of the blurred line between state and non-state control in Chinese firms. Even within CIC, there was pushback at the idea

Investment	Barclays	Blackstone Group	Morgan Stanley
Date of Purchase	Jul-07	May-07	Dec-07
Purchase Share Price	720 pence	$29.61	$48.07
Closing Share Price, 12/31/2008	153.4 pence	$6.53	$16.04
Loss from purchase to 12/31/2008	79%	78%	66%
Closing Share Price, 12/31/2010	261.65 pence	$14.15	$27.16
Loss from purchase to 12/31/2010	64%	52%	43%

Fig. 6.5 Losses on financial investments by China Development Bank and China Investment Corp. Source: Brookings John L. Thornton China Center

that it would merely do Beijing's bidding. So part of the institution was turned into a government department and part into a commercially minded investment fund.

What kind of money are these two institutions pouring into global deals? Their annual reports provide some indication. At the end of 2015, CDB had 1.3 trillion renminbi of external loans, up 7.2 percent from 2014. CDB's domestic loans had risen faster—17.74 percent—but this was still a sizable amount and growth rate (Fig. 6.6).

CIC has been less transparent. In their 2015 filing, they broke out their assets of 813.8 billion renminbi, including 722.7 billion renminbi of equity investments and financial assets. But they provided no clear statement of total overseas holdings—no doubt reflecting their humiliation from their bank losses in previous years and the National Audit Office (NAO) audit. However, there is a partial analysis in the fixed income and equity sections, which are investments in publicly tradable securities (as opposed to investments directly into private firms). Here, we can see that two-thirds of their bonds are of foreign firms, while their global equity portfolio is about evenly split between the United States and the rest of the world (Fig. 6.7).

CIC's annual returns have varied significantly over the past seven years, at times topping the average 8 percent return in US equities, while at other times losing ground. Of course, these returns are derived mainly from the bank's domestic investments so aren't necessarily relevant for analyzing international investments (Fig. 6.8).

There is a third institution that has become a growing part of China's "home team" for international deals. That is an investment company called Buttonwood, founded by State Administration of Foreign Exchange (SAFE).

Buttonwood Investment Platform was established to diversify China's foreign exchange through direct investments and targeted share purchases. In 2016, Buttonwood bought 27 billion renminbi of mainland stocks of three investment firms it controls. It is also among the top ten

	Loans (rmb bln)	Increase YoY
Total Loans	9,206	17.74%
Outside China	1,306	7.22%

Fig. 6.6 China Development Bank's loan book (2015). Source: CDB Annual Report

Fixed Income	
Sovereign Bonds of Advanced Countries	64.16%
Sovereign Bonds of Emerging Countries	5.13%
Investment Grade Corporate Bonds	30.71%
Equities	
US	46.32%
Non-US	42%
Emerging	11.68%

Fig. 6.7 China Investment Corp.: International investment portfolio (2015). Source: CIC Annual Report

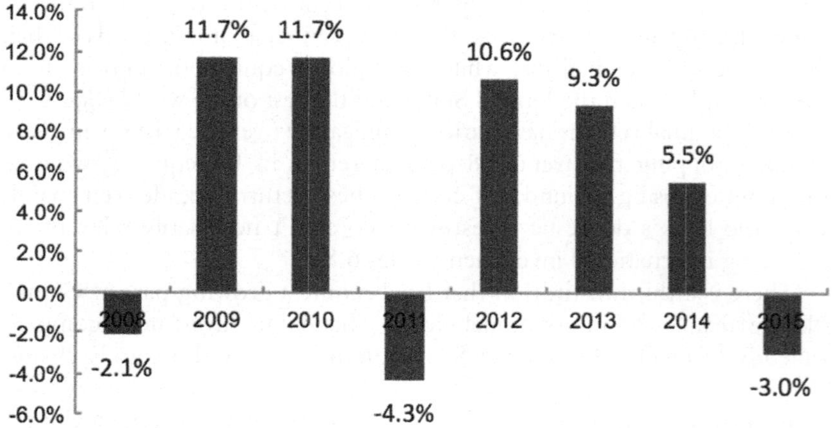

Fig. 6.8 CIC's net annual average returns. Source: CIC Annual Report

shareholders of a number of state banks, including Bank of China, Bank of Communications, and Shanghai Development Bank. Internationally, Buttonwood was SAFE's investment vehicle into China's Silk Road Fund, which was started in December 2014. The crucial point is that Beijing's leadership has been tapping all of the institutions it directly controls to fund its global leadership expansion. Buttonwood is just one among many.

ChemChina's Debt Problems

Earlier, I focused on the largest transaction from China—ChemChina's acquisition of Syngenta. This $43 billion acquisition initially fueled speculation that China was off and running on a huge spending spree. But by the time the ink had dried on the contract, many observers believed that the deal was so large and execution was so troublesome that it had scared away the authorities, the banks, ***and*** the companies themselves.

But there is another issue. Was ChemChina financially capable of paying so much for a Swiss seed firm?

In a word—no. ChemChina was in pretty poor shape to buy any company, much less one as large as Syngenta. As the chart below shows, it did not generate a profit for several years, and its returns on equity, assets, capital, and invested capital were almost all negative in 2012, 2013, and 2014. Only in 2015 and 2016 did it generate returns above nominal amounts (Fig. 6.9).

It's operating profit was fairly slim, too. ChemChina's operating margin touched 4 percent in 2015 but generally has been a lot lower—certainly lower than the median 6.7 percent of most Chinese companies (Fig. 6.10).

Another measure of ChemChina's financial position during the period of its multibillion dollar deals is cash generated after paying for basic maintenance and investment. This is called "free cash flow." This measure takes the company's cash generation, and then subtracts capital investments, to see how much actual cash is produced at the end of the day. This excludes what analysts call "non-cash" items, things like future tax payments and depreciation that have more to do with accounting practices than profits.

The company's cash from its underlying operations improved from 2012 to 2017—but it was still relatively modest, topping out only at $2.2 billion. Then, however, we have to subtract its investments, and for four years, from 2012 to 2015, the company was running in the red. Only in 2016 and 2017 did ChemChina started throwing off free cash flow. And even here it wasn't much, $756 million in 2017, far too little to give the company the financial resources to make huge overseas transactions (Fig. 6.11).

Where was the money coming from? The next chart lays out the real story. ChemChina paid for its bold acquisitions with bank debt. ChemChina's debt has soared from just over $30.4 billion in 2012 to $44.3 billion in 2017. Obviously it was borrowing heavily to pay for Syngenta—and for lots of other deals (Fig. 6.12).

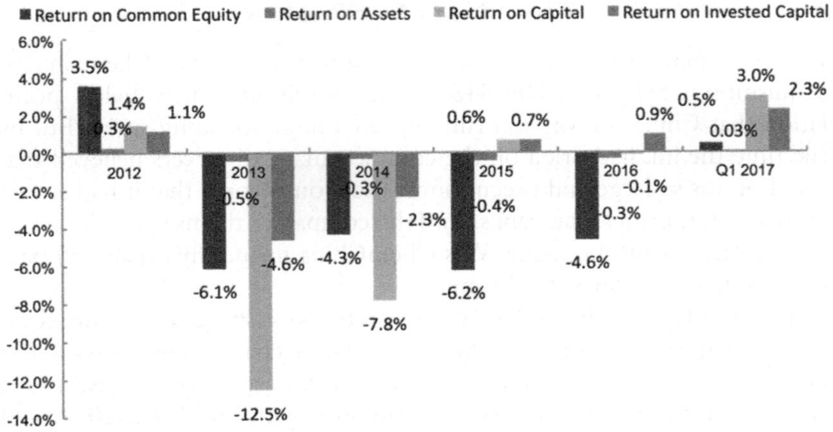

Fig. 6.9 ChemChina's profit ratios

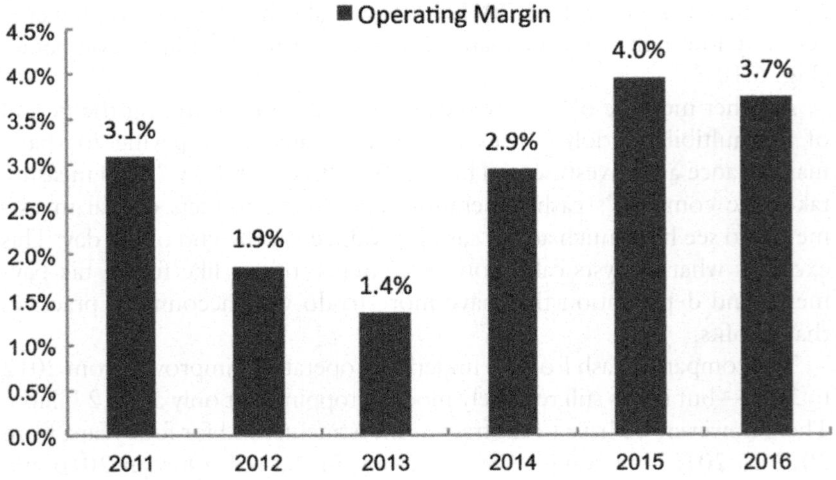

Fig. 6.10 ChemChina's operating margins. Source: Bloomberg

Shadow Banking and the Case of HNA

We have examined three methods the state can use to institute its policies: Direct ownership, political control, and access to capital. One method for sidestepping these mechanisms, at least in the capital arena, is the area of

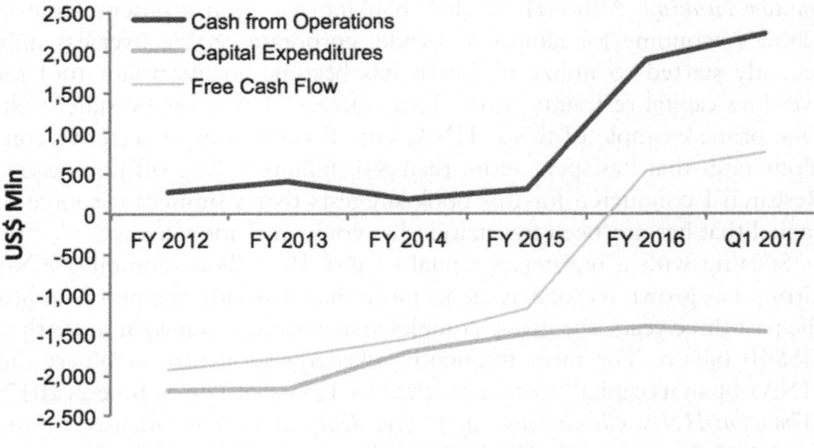

Fig. 6.11 ChemChina's Free Cash Flow. Source: Company financials, Bloomberg

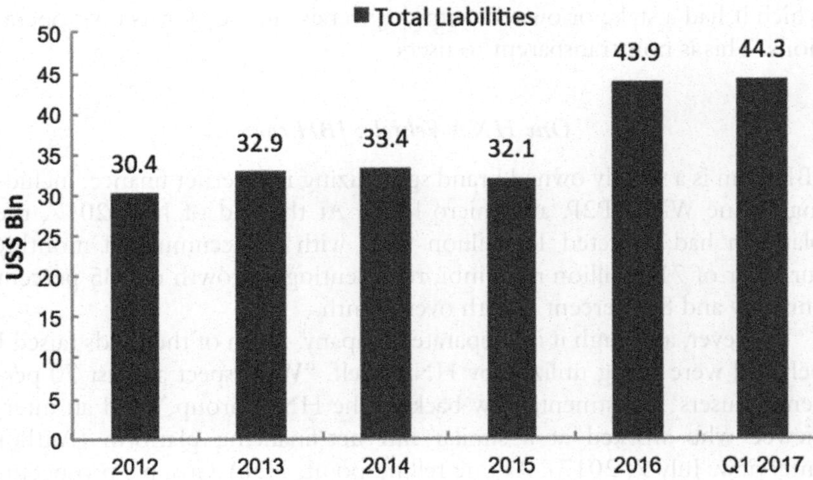

Fig. 6.12 ChemChina's debt. Source: Bloomberg

shadow banking. Although shadow banking has been a potent force in China's economy for almost a decade, corporates going overseas only recently started to utilize it. But it has become an important tool for avoiding capital restraints either from risk-wary banks or the state itself. One prime example of this is HNA, one of China's most secretive conglomerates that has spent more than $40 billion buying offshore assets. Research I conducted for this book suggests that a significant source of capital that has not been transparent has come in shadow loans.

Starting with a registered capital of just 10 million renminbi, HNA Group has grown its total assets to more than 1 trillion renminbi. In just the past three years, the group completed acquisitions valued at more than US$40 billion. The most frequently asked question now is Where did HNA obtain its capital? Recent articles (see Financial Times, June 2, 2017. *Who owns HNA, China's most aggressive dealmaker?*) have focused on the firm's early loans from the World Bank, along with offshore debt. However, I believe that much of HNA's growth was funded by off-balance sheet shadow banking loans. These loans were made through several related companies that are not detailed in any company statements.

HNA began to use third-party financial intermediaries, in many of which it had a stake or owned outright, to raise money for its own operations. This is non-transparent to users.

One HNA Vehicle: JBH.com

JBH.com is a wholly owned brand specializing in internet finance, including online WMP, P2P, and micro loans. At the end of June 2017, the platform had attracted 16 million users with an accumulated monthly turnover of 71.1 billion renminbi, representing a growth of 135 percent annually and 8.7 percent month over month.

However, although it is a separate company, much of the funds raised I believed were being utilized by HNA itself. "We suspect at least 70 percent of users' investments flow back to the HNA Group," said an interviewee who worked at a similar internet-financing platform (Author Interview, July 7, 2017). As one telling point, HNA Group's prospectus lists many subsidiaries in the online business.

Accumulated turnover of JBH reached 71.1 billion renminbi by the end of June (Fig. 6.13).

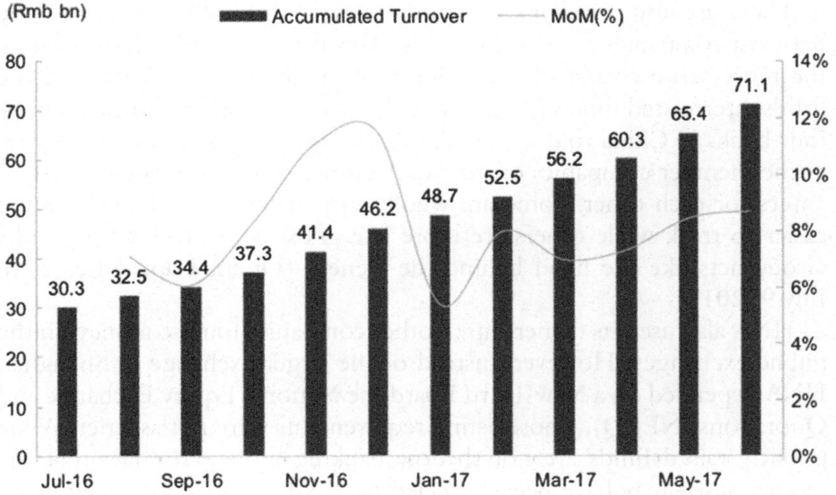

Fig. 6.13 JHB.com's Revenue Growth. Source: JBH.com; Orient Capital Research

Another Capital Source: P2P

Apart from selling investment products, JHB also had another business: P2P (peer-to-peer, which refers to a loan arranged online between two people). This is where HNA raised funds online. HNA launched its own financing products, WMPs, on at least ten P2P platforms, among which four were directly operated by HNA itself. These were JHB, lmlc, Jnzuo, and Qianhai Air & Shipping Exchange. We also believed that the HNA Group participated in two other P2P platforms, Huirendai and Weijinsuo. We couldn't find public information regarding the size or related data on the P2P platforms listed above. It is likely that the various sources of off-balance sheet funding I've detailed thus far were just the tip of the iceberg.

However, I doubted the platform itself or raising funds through WMP issuance was sustainable in the long run given that the China Banking Regulatory Commission (CBRC) has banned internal financing among online platforms. More important, consumer confidence has been severely affected by the rumor of HNA Group's difficulties raising capital. We recently interviewed a long-time JBH investor, who decided to withdraw her capital out of concerns of the risk of the investments in JBH and its connection to HNA.

There are also problems with the extensive guarantees that are made between companies for shadow loans. This occurred with HNA. One of the more serious issues this funding raises is the systemic nature of the firm's interrelated funding sources. A senior credit officer at one of the big four banks in China told us: "We're most worried about a chain reaction as the member companies of the HNA Group usually provide loan guarantees for each other. Some are wholly-owned subsidiaries and thus are easier to track while others are more like ghost companies where HNA Group acts like the hand behind-the-scenes" (Orient Capital Research, July 9, 2017).

HNA also used its ownership of other companies to raise money on the public exchanges. However, instead of the larger exchange in Shanghai, HNA depended on a New Third Board the National Equity Exchange and Quotations (NEEQ), whose listing requirements were not as strict. While publicly raised funds are not shadow banking money, the fact that the money raised may have been funneled to HNA is a form of unregulated shadow banking. As of the end of the first half of 2017, HNA had shares in approximately 18 "New Third Board" stocks, among which 14 were successfully listed and 5 were selected to join the new over-the-counter market (new OTC market) innovation board.

This funding game is not sustainable. I will discuss my predictions for shadow banking and outbound investments in the next chapter.

Bibliography

China Development Bank. 2015. *Annual Report*, P2. Beijing.

China Investment Corp. 2015. *Annual Report*, Beijing.

Le Corre, Phillip. 2016. *China's Global Rise. Can the EU and the U.S. Pursue a Coordinated Strategy*. Washington, DC: Brookings Institution.

Levine, Henry. 2017. Private correspondence with the author, August 18.

Orr and Cogman. 2017. *McKinsey: A Pocket Guide to Chinese Cross-border M&A*. China: McKinsey.

CHAPTER 7

Will China Take over the World?

Abstract What does the future hold for China's dealmaking? Will politics take command or will China allow companies to make overseas acquisitions according to capitalist principals? We discuss President Trump's policies and Xi Jinping's crackdown domestically and the effect on global corporate activity. We provide an overview of larger macroeconomic issues, including the sustainability of China's domestic property market and the future of shadow banking, and the impact these two issues will have on China's global future. We also outline possible regulatory actions that other countries can take in response to China's corporate ambitions.

Introduction

As I was writing this book, China was going through a period of turmoil. President Xi was tightening his grip on the state machinery ahead of the 19th Party Congress in the fall, which was diverting attention away from the economy and toward internecine battles in elite Chinese politics. Meanwhile, the China Banking Regulatory Commission (CBRC) and People's Bank of China (PBOC) were engaging in a series of stop-and-go policies to control credit growth and throttle financial risks in a somewhat desperate attempt to keep the engines of GDP plowing through the waves while preventing China from capsizing into a financial crisis.

A. Collier, *China Buys the World*,
https://doi.org/10.1007/978-981-10-7494-3_7

Overseas, the United States under President Donald Trump was a looming threat to China's global goals. A crisis with North Korea was pulling China against its will into a political quagmire between the two countries. Domestically, Trump's cabinet was making threatening noises about imposing sanctions against China for alleged infractions of international trade rules under the World Trade Organization (WTO). There was growing opposition in Europe toward a continued influx in corporate activity by Chinese firms. Members of European Parliament expressed concern over the real motives behind One Belt One Road (OBOR) and worried that OBOR could make Europe politically dependent on Beijing (Chaudhury 2017a).

Still, China appeared determined to push on despite the international opposition and pressing domestic issues. President Xi clearly believes that Chinese firms are an integral part of China's projection of economic, military, political, and cultural power. The twists and turns of Chinese moves make it difficult to predict the future. I have attempted to outline the underlying factors driving China's global gamble. This chapter will outline my expectations for China's corporate expansion that are likely to result from China's current political, economic, and financial trends.

China's Imperial Ambitions

One of the accusations launched at China is that it is seeking to replicate Western nations as the preeminent global power—and its corporations are merely its frontline soldiers.

Of the top 500 global corporations in *Fortune* magazine's list, China has surpassed Japan and is now number two. Among these top firms, 132 are American, while 73 are Chinese, and Japan has only 68. According to academic Michael Probsting, "In short, we see that China's monopolies are among the world's most powerful. This is yet a further indication that China has become an imperialist Great Power" (Probsting 2014).

The exploitation of foreign territories for a nation's benefit is certainly not new. This has been a recurring theme around the world for centuries. During the late eighteenth and nineteenth centuries, for example, cotton was one of the defining commodities of its era. Entire countries, including England and the United States, built their economies around the production and sale of cotton, and the control of territory related to this production. Also among them, Russia was eager to become a leading cotton producer. After Russia gained control of Central Asia in the 1860s and 1870s, the Russian government, with the backing of corporate interests, sought to use state power to replace the dominant position of the United States in global cotton production, sourced in Central Asia. They did this by investing in large infrastructure projects, similar to what China is doing now in Central Asia, Southeast Asia, and Africa. Russian colonial bureaucrat Shtaba L. Kostenko commanded that "the aim of all of our efforts has to be the striving to remove from our inner markets the American cotton and to replace it with our own, Central Asian one." To make this possible, the colonial administration undertook large-scale infrastructure projects, such as the building of railroads (Beckert 2014).

As Sven Beckert, author of "Empire of Cotton," noted: "The newfound ability of capitalists and states to transform the global cotton-growing countryside with the tools of industrial capitalism allowed for ever more cotton to arrive at ever cheaper prices in the ports of Liverpool, Bremen, Le Havre, Osaka, and Boston" (Beckert 2014). Is this what China is doing?

As I have attempted to describe in this book, China's companies have a mixed relationship with the state. This was apparent during the 2017 crackdown on overseas investments by Wanda, HNA, and several other firms. They were accused of "asset transfer," which was an internal code name for misusing domestic assets for personal corporate gain. But who's to say exactly why HNA paid $6.5 billion for a 25 percent stake in Hilton Hotels? Was this merely a way to move money offshore before the Chinese economy collapsed? Or was it a genuine effort to extend the China brand into the world's biggest hotel market?

It is perhaps relatively easy for an organization like Committee on Foreign Investment in the US (CFIUS) to point to a Chinese purchase of a defense contractor and say that it clearly improves China's military. However, it's more difficult to say that machine learning and artificial intelligence are primarily military technologies, as Congress at one point was prodding the Trump administration to do (Stewart 2007).

China, ultimately, wants its companies to become global giants. The problem is that it is hard for the officials in Beijing to achieve this goal while restraining companies that are using their power to move money overseas—with no benefits to anyone but themselves. At a time of worries about currency reserves, this has been a big red flag.

This is one of the reasons why in 2017 Beijing cracked down so harshly on five companies, which caused a decline in the size of overall transactions. "The level of contracts is way down because they are so much smaller. The deals China ultimately cares about are the big ones. They need to figure out how to regulate them. The China dream can't be achieved without the big deals," said one Beijing lawyer involved in international transactions (Author interview, June 2, 2017).

It is difficult to clearly distinguish between "legitimate" state interests and corporate greed. However, this book's goal is to provide the tools to analyze the complexity of China's corporate ambitions.

A Quick Take on Future Trends

There are certain trends that leap out as I look at what the future holds for outbound China mergers and acquisitions (M&A).

- **Growth.** First of all, despite all the political and economic uncertainties roiling in China, foreign investment is likely to grow. One important way to look at this is to compare China with other nations. According to a McKinsey study, Chinese companies spent 0.9 percent of GDP on outbound acquisitions in 2015: the US companies spent 1.3 percent, and EU companies 2.0 percent, investing 2.4× and 3.2× the dollar amount Chinese companies spent. Assuming China follows in the footsteps of some of its larger international brethren, there is plenty of room to grow (McKinsey 2017, p. 18). However, as we discuss further, there is likely to be a hiccup in growth due to the difficulty in obtaining financing.
- **Smaller Deals.** Second, it's likely that future transactions will be smaller. China is losing its risk-taking appetite and is clearly no longer willing to hand over blank checks to any corporate CEO—private or state-owned enterprise (SOE)—who declares an ambition to rush overseas. The largest, most visible transactions tend to attract attention both within China and abroad. This is against the wishes of the Chinese government, which would prefer that its ambitions, intentions, and methods do not raise red flags internationally.
- **Strategic Focus.** Third, there will be an emphasis on transactions strategic for China. The biggest deals (apart from Syngenta) in 2017 were in media and real estate, two areas that the state later deemed non-strategic and merely vehicles for overseas asset transfers. China will, instead, continue to push for acquisitions in technology and advanced industries that increase the country's place in the global economy.

- **More Profitable Transactions.** Chinese firms are becoming more sophisticated, hiring lawyers and consultants and performing economic analysis on target companies. Those transactions—especially smaller ones that don't end up in any strategic buckets—will be driven increasingly by economic logic. That doesn't mean there won't be more port build-outs as we have seen in Sri Lanka. But the bulk of the transactions will be profitable. In 2017, the median deal size has not been that large—just $30 million—with the Syngenta- and Wanda-type acquisitions representing outliers.
- **Split Between Large and Small.** The increasing focus in the Chinese state on large-scale corporates, coupled with an expected decline in informal lending, will create a division between big, state-driven SOE acquisitions and smaller, private deals.

One example of the aggressive behavior of smaller Chinese firms has occurred in the Netherlands. There, Chinese investment is dominated by small, private firms, with 75 percent of the investment non-state owned. More than three-quarters of the firms employ fewer than five people with 41 percent employing only one staff member (raising questions of whether these are actual investments or merely moving money offshore) (Dejong 2017).

However, there are two broader issues that may determine the future of China's overseas push: the political campaign against some of the country's top dealmakers and a potential shortfall in funding that could rein in their ambitions.

The Political Crackdown

In the middle of 2017, China suddenly turned cold on five companies. The CBRC quietly asked these top firms for information about their deals that had gone astray as part of an examination of risks to the financial sector. The five firms involved were Anbang Insurance Group Co., Dalian Wanda Group Co., Fosun International Ltd., HNA Group Co., and the Chinese buyer of the AC Milan soccer club. Among the questions asked were the likelihood of litigation costs, potential losses to banks, and whether there was adequate due diligence. These investigations showed the vacillating policy about China's global corporate expansion—and the tensions within China's political system.

While there may have been political factors, the broader issue was whether these acquisitions forwarded China's strategic goals. One comment was made by a research analyst for the State Council on China's CCTV, considered the mouthpiece for the government in Beijing and generally viewed as an official statement.

The analyst said five sectors were targeted as "irrational outbound investment": property, hotels, cinema, entertainment, and soccer clubs. Many overseas transactions are "not real … they are de facto asset transfers," CCTV said, quoting the research analyst. "They were not meant to invest money [for profit] but to move assets abroad," said Yin Zhongli, who works for the Chinese Academy of Social Sciences, which is affiliated with the State Council. Asset transfer is Beijing's euphemism for a loss of national wealth (SCMP, July 17, 2017). In one example, property developer Wanda was told by its banks that it could not obtain loans to be used for overseas transactions.

However, other officials said that good transactions would be permitted to go ahead. "There was an outstanding problem of irrational outbound investment by a few companies last year, so we worked with other regulators to determine if the deals were genuine," according to vice-commerce minister Qian Keming. "The irrational investment has now been effectively curbed" (SCMP, August 2, 2017).

David Dollar of the Brookings Institution in Washington stated it this way: "the new restrictions announced by China on its companies investing abroad reflect both the country's macroeconomic policy as well as its industrial policy. China wants an overall outflow of capital that leaves reserves and the exchange rate stable. It also wants to micro-manage the outflow to favor hi-tech, natural resources and construction of infrastructure" (Dollar, August 23, 2017).

The crackdown suggested that in future, China had some ability to control the flow of deals through the banking system. Certainly, there was a slowdown in late 2016 and early 2017 in the frenzied pace of activity (Fig. 7.1).

We can see the impact of the policies on deal flow—particularly to the United States, because there were concerns within China about CFIUS security investigations. The US investments fell a substantial 82 percent in the first seven months of 2017 (Fig. 7.2).

However, as I discussed earlier, China is not a monolith; it is a country of many moving parts—and sources of funding. I have talked a bit about how Chinese corporates evade political and economic controls. These can take many forms: "regulatory arbitrage" in which corporate actors find

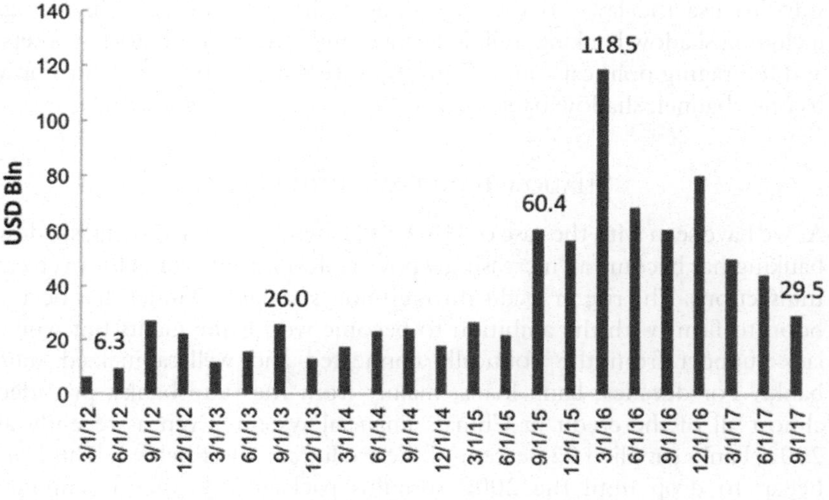

Fig. 7.1 Value of China Outbound Deals. Source: Bloomberg

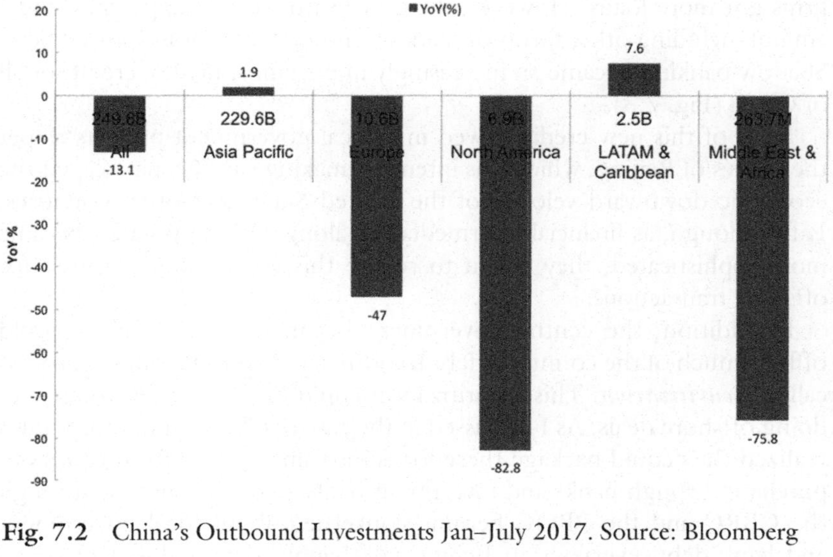

Fig. 7.2 China's Outbound Investments Jan–July 2017. Source: Bloomberg

ways to use the laws to their advantage; alternate forms of financing, including shadow banking, online finance, and misuse of the stock markets; and leveraging political connections to move money offshore. I turn now to one channel: shadow banking.

Shadow Banking's End Game

As we have seen with the case of HNA and ChemChina/Syngenta, shadow banking has become an increasingly powerful source of capital for overseas transactions. The rise in credit through non-standard channels has been a boon to firms with the ambition to become worldwide giants but which lack support from the politically connected and well-capitalized state banks. For decades, bank loans, mainly from the state banks, provided almost all of the credit in China's financial system. Even as recently as 2002, banks supplied 92 percent of the credit (see chart below). This level began to drop until the 2009 stimulus package's 4 trillion renminbi poured into the economy like water over a dam. Total credit doubled from 6.9 trillion renminbi in 2008 to 13.9 trillion renminbi in 2009. As a result, bank loans dropped from 70 percent of the total in 2008 to 57 percent in 2010. Bank loans as a share of the total increased slightly in 2015 as state firms got more loans. However, the downward trend is apparent—and I am not including other forms of shadow lending that is not captured here. Shadow banking became an increasingly important source of credit for all of China (Fig. 7.3).

Most of this new credit flowed into local government projects as per the wishes of Beijing, which was intent on making sure China escaped the economic downward velocity of the United States and other countries. Later, though, as financial intermediaries, along with corporates, became more sophisticated, they began to realize this credit could be used for offshore transactions.

In addition, the central government began to realize that it could offload much of the country's debt to ordinary citizens through a process called *securitization*. This securitization could be utilized by companies doing offshore deals. As I discussed in the case of ChemChina, corporates realized they could package these loans into small pieces for investors to purchase through banks and investment banks—securitization. Although the CBRC and the PBOC became concerned about local government and bank debt, everyone in Beijing was happy to shift this debt on to consumers in the form of securitized shadow banking loans (mainly wealth management products, WMPs).

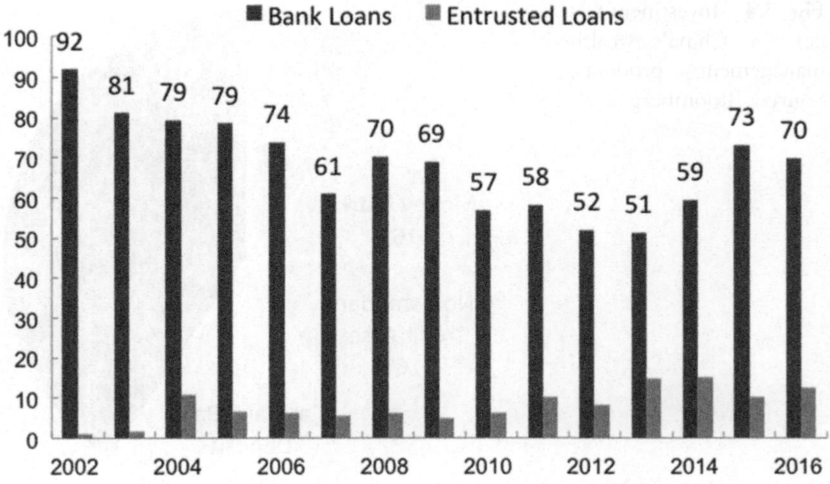

Fig. 7.3 China's Shadow Banking Loans. Source: Wang et al. 2017

There is virtually no data on how much shadow credit has been funneled into overseas transactions. The China Trustee Association collects information on the assets that are amassed by the country's 67 trusts, which are considered to be shadow banks. However, that data only provides information on investments in tradable instruments such as bonds and stocks and does not detail where the capital eventually ends up, domestically or overseas.

Similarly, the data for another major category, 27 trillion renminbi in WMPs in the middle of 2017, is also quite vague. The most detail we have comes from announcements relating to specific transactions, such as with Syngenta. There, we saw that ChemChina and its banks sought to offload a significant portion of their debt on to private investors. This trend appears to be increasing.

More generally, we can also look at the data on the investment target for WMPs. The largest area is bonds, accounting for 40 percent of the total. This is followed by cash (18 percent), non-standard credit assets (16 percent), money market (16 percent), and equities (10 percent).

In terms of funding for foreign transactions by Chinese corporations, the two of interest are bonds and non-standard credit assets. Bonds are sold by corporates (and governments), and non-standard assets are often

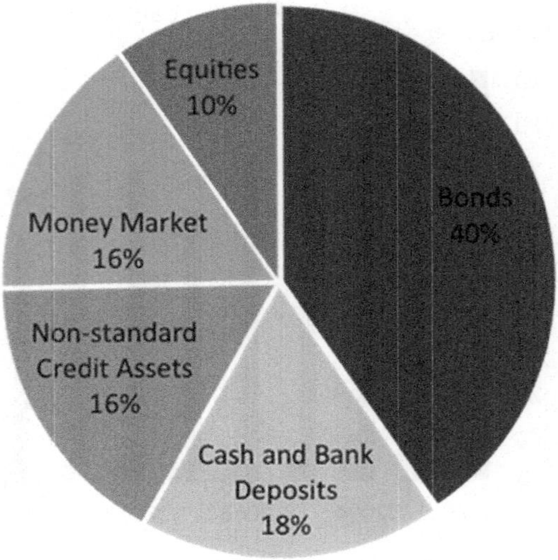

Fig. 7.4 Investment target for China's wealth management products. Source: Bloomberg

direct investments in resources or corporations that bypass the securities markets (which is why they are called "non-standard.") Combined, they accounted for a little over half, or about 14 trillion renminbi, of the outstanding WMPs as of mid-2017. Bear in mind that these loans—which is basically what they are, although dressed up in other formats—have fewer checks and balances than bank loans. These WMPs have been a contributing source of capital for companies to use for whatever purpose they deem of interest—such as international transactions. However, it is almost impossible to pin down the amount of credit available to internationally acquisitive companies that was sourced from the unofficial capital markets (Fig. 7.4).

We did note earlier that another firm, HNA Group, had sourced a significant amount of capital from shadow loans. Bloomberg estimated that it is in billions of dollars (Bloomberg, August 25, 2017).

However, the bigger point is that shadow credit is likely to decline in the future as the massive amount of excess investments fails to generate returns adequate to pay cost of interest. A run on WMPs alone would cause 27 trillion renminbi in credit to disappear overnight. This would cause difficulties for corporates looking to raise capital on the private shadow markets outside of the exchanges or the banks.

We can see this in specific companies. In the middle of 2017, the debt load created by China's largest corporations increasingly looked like it was going to hinder their ability to continue at the same pace of overseas acquisitions. And this debt included shadow loans. Four of the top corporate dealmakers were scheduled to pay back at least $11.5 billion in bonds and loans by the end of 2018. This was debt owed by HNA Group, Fosun International, Dalian Wanda, and Anbang.

One expected outcome was the likely increase in the cost of borrowing for these aggressive firms. "We anticipate that yield levels for bonds from companies like HNA, Dalian Wanda and Fosun could rise in the near term," said Anne Zhang, executive director for fixed income, currencies, and commodities at JPMorgan Private Bank in Asia. By the middle of 2017, this was already beginning to happen. HNA Group was seeking shadow lends for 4.5 billion renminbi, offering rates as high as 7 percent (Bloomberg, July 5, 2017).

What would happen if debt constraints reached more of China's companies? Interest rates would rise on bank loans—and most likely skyrocket on the more liquid, market-oriented shadow loans. This would spell trouble for China's dealmakers.

The Global Real Estate Gamble

One of the most ambitious—and politically fraught—industries in China's global sweepstakes has been the property industry. For years, if not decades, China's property companies have turned into some of the largest and most aggressive players in the country. The reason was simple: in China, property is not just a place to live. It's also a store of value, a kind of giant piggy bank at a time when China has offered few other, safe, investment options. The stock market is a casino, torn by insider trading and high-level government connections; the bond market is still in its infancy although growing fast (partly due to property developers); and there is only the beginnings of a pool of retirement savings that is professionally managed, mainly because there is nowhere to invest on the scale that Westerners are accustomed to. What's left is property.

The other key reason the property companies have flourished in China is that, for nearly a decade starting in 2008 during the financial crisis, there has been an incredible boom in lending. To stimulate the economy, and feed revenue-short local governments, China created a large financial industry adept at turning savings into investments. Much of this capital has gone into the property sector. Property has been nearly a one-way bet for homeowners and developers alike since at least the early 2000s, and especially since 2008.

Not surprisingly, Chinese developers, awash in profits, in 2015 started to hungrily eye overseas markets. They also were prompted by overconstruction of homes in China, slowing GDP growth, and concerns about the strength of the currency. Soon, the developers announced a flurry of transactions. As I stated earlier, Anbang (an insurance firm with an interest in property) acquired the Waldorf Astoria Hotel in 2015 for $2 billion and later put forward an aborted bid for the Starwood Hotel chain. The HNA conglomerate, with its tentacles in many industries, acquired a 25 percent stake in the Hilton Hotels chain.

In some ways, the biggest push came not from the large developers but from individual Chinese interested in moving their money offshore. Chinese investment in residential property was $93 billion between 2010 and 2015, while commercial property took in $17.1 billion, according to a report by the Asia Society in New York (Asia Society, May 2016).

If we look forward to the future of this flood of Chinese capital into foreign homes, hotels, and other construction, there are two conflicting trends. First, our contention is that continued political instability, coupled with declining GDP growth, will encourage capital flight. And for most Chinese, owning a piece of real estate is the safest investment. This applies to both big developers and individual homeowners. However, the second trend I forecast will be negative for overseas property investments. A shortage of capital will force the country's leaders to become more selective about who will have access to it. We've already seen this gradual capital hoarding in the case of foreign exchange, where offshore deals have been tightly scrutinized since 2016. This capital shortage will play out against rising headwinds in the domestic property market that will be an additional crimp in the developers' freewheeling ways.

First, I believe there is a housing glut in China—despite rising prices at the time of writing in mid-2017—and this has been taken on board by the property companies. While there is a debate about how much of a bubble China's property market is in, there are many skeptics. Some data supports this view.

In 2017, Zhu Yunlai (Levin Zhu), son of former Chinese Premier Zhu Rongji and a prominent investment banker, published a scathing commentary on the dire state of China's property market. As he noted in his widely viewed article,

China's current total housing capacity can supply 1 billion people, at an average rate of 30 square meters per person. Counting even people living in small towns, China has only 700 million urban dwellers. That means there is a 300 million over-capacity. The nationwide average housing price is 7,000 yuan (US $1,000) per square meter. The average income for urban residents is 30,000 yuan per year. Taking out expenses and taxes, 10,000 yuan can be used for house payments. The housing price has way exceeded the general public's purchasing capability. Then why are houses so expensive? It is because of the financial factor. China has issued 160 trillion yuan. The number is still rising. So the housing price for sure is rising—that's called asset inflation. (Chinascope, July 12, 2017)

Growth in sales, completions, and investments is slowing. I think this reflects either a funding gap for heavily indebted developers or concerns about the future of the property market itself. Given that household and mortgage loans keep climbing, there certainly appeared to be little appetite in Beijing to restrain the property market. There is a powerful lobby among local government officials to keep the sector alive as it comprises at least 40 percent of local government revenue (Fig. 7.5).

Fig. 7.5 Floor space YoY %

Fig. 7.6 Property Industry Investments

The property industry's investments, although slowing, have been quite high (Fig. 7.6)

Debt Remains a Problem for Developers

Parking money overseas is one way to avoid the downturn. But will the developers have the capital to do it? Chinese developers have added debt by an average of 23 percent per year over the last five years, and in 2017 their debt topped 1 trillion renminbi, or about $150 billion dollars (Fig. 7.7).

In addition, desperate to keep their lending costs down, in 2017 property developers engaged in a particularly risky form of borrowing: puttable bonds. A puttable bond allows the buyer to demand early repayment. So instead of borrowing money for a long period of time, adequate to get the building up and running, developers lowered their cost of capital by selling bonds that they could be forced to repay *almost at any time*. At the time of writing in late 2017, approximately 20 percent of outstanding domestic corporate bonds took this form, compared with 4 percent globally.

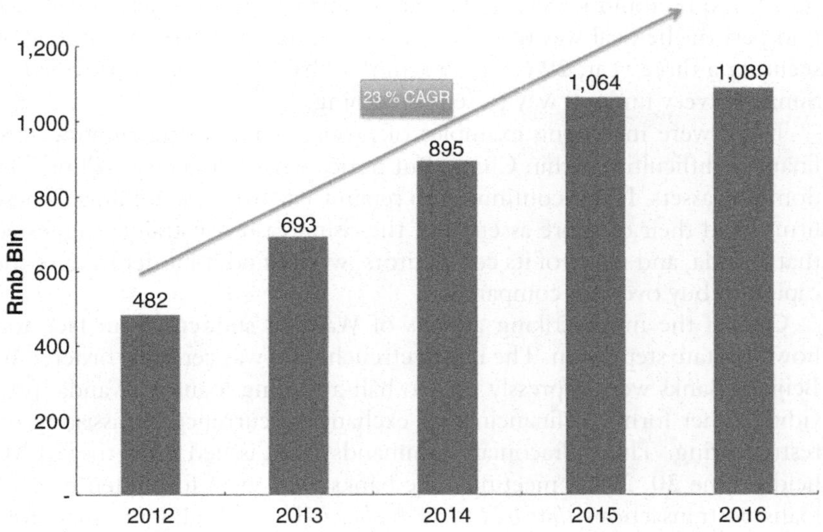

Fig. 7.7 Property Developer Debt

That was a total of $420 billion, almost double the $233 billion in puttable bonds elsewhere in the world. More than half of these bonds were issued by real estate developers.

> The number of puts becoming exercisable will peak in 2018 and 2019, which gives issuers time to plan for refinancing. This makes it unlikely that puts will be a cause of systemic stress. However, puts will shift forward the funding needs of some companies, and are likely to push up the cost of debt-servicing earlier than some companies had planned. Isolated problems cannot be ruled out, with companies that are heavily reliant on puttable bonds likely to face pressure in the event of a significant tightening of liquidity conditions. (Lai 2017)

It was becoming increasingly clear that financial stress had struck many property developers. In China, there was a rumor that Wanda's banks had called some of the company's loans, so it had to find a buyer for some of its assets—within one week. In July 2017, Sunac China Holdings Ltd. agreed to buy hotels, land, and projects from Dalian Wanda Group Co. for

63.2 billion renminbi ($9.3 billion) in China's largest property deal. The odd part of the deal was that Wanda was providing half of the money by securing a three-year, 29.6 billion renminbi bank loan that it provided to Sunac—a very unusual way to sell something.

There were increasing examples of property developers running into financial difficulties within China. But notice what Wanda was selling—its domestic assets. It was continuing to retain to its overseas holdings. These firms liked their offshore assets. But the rising cash constraints suggested that Wanda, and many of its competitors, would find it harder to raise the capital to buy overseas companies.

One of the most striking aspects of Wanda's sudden about-face was how the state stepped in. The rapid retrenchment was certainly ordered by Beijing. Banks were expressly told to halt awarding loans to Wanda, providing other forms of financing, or exchanging currency, or assisting on restructuring. These draconian commands were issued after the CBRC held a June 20, 2017, meeting. The banks were even forbidden to issue loans on transactions *that had already closed*. This is highly unusual, even for China's politics-ridden financial system (SCMP, July 17, 2017).

At the time of writing, it was not clear how Wanda would be able to complete the contracts it had already signed. It was unlikely that China would allow Wanda to back out of signed contracts as that would be an embarrassment for China globally and hurt the country's ability to arrange contracts in the future. But it was clear its days of overseas expansion were over.

However, there was a new plot twist. Just before publication, there was a debate over the estimates of overseas property investments. Despite the backlash against developers, there may have been a significant increase in property investment—but obscured by confusing data. The official data showed an 82 percent decline in outbound real estate investment in the first half of 2017. However, a report by a private company, CBRE, said real estate spending actually *grew* 102 percent. The difference was accounted for by capital spent that was already offshore and therefore didn't show up in the totals for outbound deals. Furthermore, while SOE investments fell 66 percent, purchases by China's policy banks soared by 19-fold, in part due to a large acquisition in Europe. The CBRE said these policy banks are not subject to capital controls because they have a special status in China's hierarchy (Caixin, August 24, 2017).

This is further evidence that Beijing policy matters—but only up to a point. There are always exceptions and ways around the rules. In this case, the policy banks and many private developers found those loopholes.

The CBRC data also points to another key fact—there is a great deal of Chinese capital already offshore that can be utilized for transactions. This capital comes either from offshore profits or through intracompany and other transfers. There is little data on how much of this money there is. But it will make government attempts to control transactions that much harder.

Tightening Circle of Capital

As noted earlier, McKinsey is optimistic that Chinese outbound acquisitions will grow because they currently represent just 0.9 percent of GDP compared with 1.3 percent of GDP in the United States and 2 percent in Europe. That may be true—long term. In the near term, though, I believe there will be significant restraints, partly due to capital considerations.

China has been a significant overseas lender. Banks in China reported $778 billion in cross-border claims in June 2016, according to the Bank for International Settlements. In addition, as of 2014, Chinese bank branches outside the mainland were estimated to have $1 trillion in offshore assets at the end of 2014. "Chinese banks are very much integrating into global banking markets" (BIS, June 2017).

Despite these loans, China's global ambitions may run into the simple roadblock of lack of capital and a large amount of existing debt. The huge growth of credit through formal and informal sources has provided the monetary underpinnings of corporate acquisitions. It may be difficult for China to maintain this pace in the future.

Even McKinsey acknowledges there could be a pause, although they believe it would be temporary.

> Rising interest rates in the developed world and an eventual tightening of credit in China will, in time, rein this back somewhat, as will recent Chinese government talk of slowing down outbound M&A to reduce the risk of capital flight. However the banks – Chinese and foreign – are simply responding to the needs of Chinese companies, and their interest in outbound acquisitions will only grow in the coming years. (McKinsey, April 2017)

I am not sure I agree with this optimistic assessment of China's future corporate expansion, at least for the next few years.

One of the problems is that Chinese firms have significant amounts of debt. Chinese firms that announced transactions in the first seven months of 2017 had $422 billion of debt, according to Bloomberg data. However, some companies are not publicly traded and don't report their financials, so the total amount of debt is certainly much higher.

Slowing Pace of Loans: A Cautionary Signal

Already, there has been a sharp decline starting in 2014 of new loans in foreign currencies issued by Chinese banks. They fell from a monthly peak of 916 billion renminbi at the end of 2012 to a net redemption of 564 billion renminbi in 2016 (Fig. 7.8).

Similarly, there's also been a decline in the issuance of foreign bonds by Chinese companies. These bonds hit a peak of 213 billion renminbi in 2016, but fell to just 36.7 billion renminbi in the first three months of 2017 (Fig. 7.9).

The decline in foreign loans may reflect controls by State Administration of Foreign Exchange (SAFE) over relatively scarce foreign exchange.

Fig. 7.8 Foreign Currency Loans. Source: Bloomberg

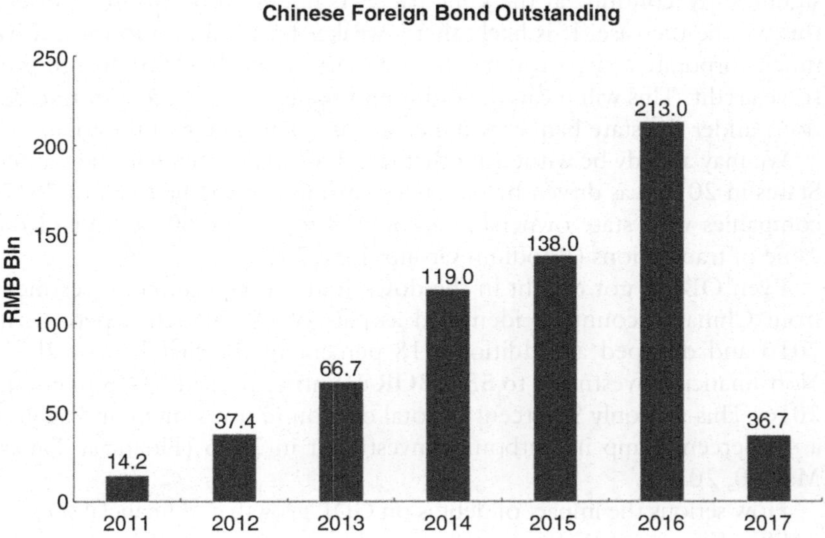

Fig. 7.9 Foreign Bond Issuance. Source: Bloomberg

However, these foreign-currency-denominated bonds are purchased by foreigners using external capital and thus are free of the SAFE controls. Admittedly, Chinese corporates may have envisioned a depreciation of the Chinese currency, which would make it more expensive to repay foreign debt.

Access to capital will also be a function of the nature of the firm doing the deal. Obviously, firms with political connections will have an easier time accessing bank loans than private firms. In difficult times, when profits decline, private firms that have been making significant offshore purchases will slow their expansion plans. As one academic study noted, "examining the role of government connections via CEO appointments, we find that investment is more sensitive to cash flows in firms with non-government-appointed CEOs than those with government-appointed CEOs…our findings suggest that large, non-state, unconnected firms may be especially financially constrained" (Federal Reserve, January 2015).

If their findings are correct, that means the shadow banking market will remain an important source of funding for future outbound acquisitions, particularly for private firms. But will this funding, which has grown significantly, continue at the same pace? As discussed previously, I doubt this will be the case. It is likely that a weaker financial position will drive much corporate activity toward the state sector, which will be able to preserve credit. This will mean the outbound figure of 56 percent of transactions under the state banner will increase as a percentage of the total.

We may already be witnessing that trend. China's activity in the United States in 2016 was driven by private companies. In the first half of 2017, companies with state ownership accounted for nearly 60 percent of the value of transactions (Rhodium Group, June 2017).

Even OBOR got caught in the downdraft. Foreign direct investment from China to countries identified as part of OBOR fell 2 percent in 2016 and dropped an additional 18 percent in the first half of 2017. Non-financial investment to 53 OBOR countries totaled $14.5 billion in 2016. This was only 9 percent of total outbound investment and against a 40 percent jump in outbound investment in 2016 (Financial Times, May 10, 2017).

How serious the impact of debt is on GDP growth and financial stability is difficult to assess. Economists debate this question. Can China beat the odds, overcome its debt, approaching 300 percent of GDP, and avoid a financial crisis? Charlene Chu, a former employee of the Federal Reserve and independent analyst, employed a method that looks at the waste of capital. She examined how much investment was required to generate average GDP growth. Historically, for every 1 yuan, the country generated 0.73 in new GDP. However, that ratio fell drastically by 2016 to just 0.18. So for the two years of 2016 and into 2017, she estimated that China would be estimated to waste 109 trillion renminbi in inefficient investments, or 49 percent of outstanding credit. This is essentially just all bad debt. It will be difficult for China to support corporate expansion if it is busy fighting losses of that size on its loans (Autonomous Research, July 2017).

Ultimately, the state's decisions on global acquisitions may be a matter of dealing with the hard reality of lack of capital—not policy.

How to Control China?

How should the world's nations respond to China? I have tried to stress that the Chinese government in Beijing is not in control of all of the economy and the country may have resource problems in the future. Beyond this, there are specific recommendations for countries seeking to strike a balance between the benefits of Chinese investment and the dangers of loss of national control over important assets. One of the better responses comes from Columbia University's Curtis Milhaupt. He argues that the United States and other countries can create adequate protection for key assets by *accurately* defining the parameters of analysis. Foreign countries must examine the *specifics* of transactions. In other words broad-brush policies won't work. His list includes the following factors:

- First, does the federal securities law disclosure regime provide investors with a complete and accurate picture of the ownership and governance of Chinese SOEs?
- Second, is the antitrust regime equipped to accurately assess the competitive effects of SOE behavior in US markets? What is the relevant unit of analysis in considering market effects of SOE conduct—a specific firm, the business group to which that firm belongs, or a number of groups under common control of a state shareholder?
- Third, what is the proper scope of investment treaties to which the United States is a party? Bilateral investment treaties (BITs) generally provide for investor-state, but not state-state, dispute resolution. When an investment is made by a state-owned or state-controlled enterprise, should that entity be characterized as an "investor" for purposes of the treaty, such that a dispute relating to the investment falls within the scope of the BIT's procedures? Or is the dispute more properly characterized as state-state and thus outside the scope of the BIT?

This is only a beginning laundry list for how other nations should confront the Chinese corporate tidal wave. There are many ways of addressing these investments. The main point is that creating policy responses to China without understanding how China functions is like fielding a baseball team without first checking the other team's lineup. It can only lead to failed plays.

One other issue that cropped up just as I was putting this book to bed is party control within foreign firms. According to a *Reuters* report,

> One senior executive whose company was represented at the meeting told Reuters some companies were under "political pressure" to revise the terms of their joint ventures with state-owned partners to allow the party final say over business operations and investment decisions. He said the company's joint venture partner was pushing to amend their agreement to include language

> mandating party personnel be "brought into the business management organization", that "party organization overhead expenses shall be included in the company budget", and that posts of board chairman and party secretary be held by the same person. Changing joint venture agreement terms is the main concern, the executive said, noting that his company had thus far resisted. (Martina 2017)

This obviously drew the consternation of European corporate executives in China. It is doubtful they would permit Chinese influence over important decisions. But once again, they would have to draw lines in an area that is gray.

Summary

China has had a tumultuous history since the post-Mao period that began in 1949, including the famine of the 1950s, the political dissolution of the Cultural Revolution in the 1960s, and nascent capitalism in the 1980s. Since the country's entry into the WTO, the world has witnessed China's unparalleled growth. Therefore, given the country's ups and downs, rather than make hard predictions, I have attempted to point out the underlying themes that will dictate China's overseas corporate activity. I can summarize a few of our main themes.

- **State-Private Conflict.** The state has a mixed relationship with the private sector. There will be a tug and pull in the financial system between the poles of market capitalism and state control. Market capitalism has made significant inroads in overseas acquisitions. I expect this to continue as Beijing seeks to maintain control of a fast-moving corporate bus. There will be an increasing split between these two poles. Rising opposition from the West will force China to clarify the distinction between state and private sector foreign investments. This should make it easier for foreign nations to make decisions about the nature of Chinese acquisitions.
- **Financial Realities.** There are limits on China's ability to fund growth through debt. These limits at some point in the near future will impact corporate activity. I suspect that private firms will be the losers in accessing capital. We have seen the limits of shadow banking, and the escalation of risk in the financial system. These forces will curtail outward expansion. My belief is that large SOEs will continue to expand internationally with the support of state and policy banks, while the private outbound flows will be dominated by smaller

companies. These will struggle for capital as state banks tighten lending and the growth of shadow banking flattens out.
- **State Goals.** Beijing will continue to promote acquisitions that forward its strategic goals, including security, technology, and raw materials. But not all acquisitions should be seen as state-directed.

I have not addressed in detail the response of the recipient countries as that is not the focus of my book. However, there is growing opposition to China's dealmaking. This, clearly, will force China to reevaluate and adjust how its corporates will attempt to expand their global profile. China is adept at switching strategies but sometimes it cannot control its own actors.

How this careful dance plays out—between China's ambitions and resources and the political will of the world's countries—will be one of the most important issues for global economic growth.

Bibliography

Beckert, Sven. 2014. Ch11. *Empire of Cotton*. New York: Random House.

Chaudhury, Dipanjan. 2017a. European MPs Caution OBOR Could Make Continent Subservient to China. *Economic Times*, May 6, Brussels.

———. 2017b. China May Hit Funds Roadblock Over OBOR, Think Tank Says. *Economic Times*, May 30, New Delhi.

Corman, David, et al. 2017. *A Pocket Guide to Chinese Cross-border M&A*. Shanghai: Mckinsey China.

Dejong, Piter. 2017. Getting the Numbers Right on China's Actual Overseas Investment: The Case of the Netherlands. *Journal of Current Chinese Affairs* 46 (1): 187–209.

Lai, Wayne. 2017. *Heavy Reliance on Puttable Bonds Poses Funding Risks for Some Chinese Firms*. Fitch Ratings: Hong Kong. June 28.

Martina, Michael. 2017. In China, the Party's Push for Influence Inside Foreign Firms Stirs Fears. *Reuters*, August 24, Beijing.

Probsting, Michael. 2014. China's Emergence as an Imperial Power. *New Politics*, XV-1, Summer, Brooklyn.

Stewart, Phil. 2007. U.S. Weighs Restricting Chinese Investment in Artificial Intelligence. *Reuters*, Washington, DC.

Wang, Hao, et al. 2017. *Shadow Banking: China's Dual-Track Interest Rate Liberalization*. Beijing: Tsinghua University School of Economics and Management.

Bibliography

Anbang's Big Adventure. 2015. *Caixin*, January 30, Beijing.

Anbang Insurance Group. 2017. Official Website Access http://www.anbang-group.com/jtjs/index.htm

Anderlini, Jamil. 2014a. Chinese Fund CIC Under Fire Over Overseas Losses. *Financial Times*, June 18, London.

Anderlini, James. 2014b. Chinese Fund CIC Under Fire Over Overseas Losses. *Financial Times*, June 18, Beijing.

Bath, Vivienne. 2012. *China Companies and Investment—The Balance Between Domestic and International Concerns*, July. Society of International and Economic Law. Singapore: SIEL Conference.

Beckert, Sven. 2014. Ch11. *Empire of Cotton*. New York: Random House.

Billionaire. 2017. Author Interview. May 7.

Bloomberg. 2017a. Company Overview of Anbang Insurance Group Co., Ltd.

———. 2017b. *China's $246 Billion Foreign Buying Spree Is Unraveling*. New York: Bloomberg. May 15.

Bloomberg News. 2016. Cited in *South China Morning Post*, February 4.

———. 2017. *Beijing Mulls Relaxing Controls on Insurers' Offshore Investments*, June 29, Beijing.

Book Review. 2015. Markets Over Mao. *Asia Policy* 20: 143–168.

Bradsher, Keith. 2017. Anbang's Sales Dry Up in New Challenge for Chinese Insurers. *New York Times*, June 15, New York.

Brown, David. 2016. *PWC M&A 2016 Midyear Review and Outlook*. Hong Kong: PWC. August 10.

China Development Bank. 2015. *Annual Report*. Levine, Henry. Senior Director, Stonebridge International.

———. p. 45.

A. Collier, *China Buys the World*,
https://doi.org/10.1007/978-981-10-7494-3

CFIUS. Website. Accessed at https://www.treasury.gov/resource-center/international/Pages/Committee-on-Foreign-Investment-in-US.aspx

Chatrong, Wichita. 2017. China's Loan Terms Rejected. *The Nation*, August 14, Bangkok.

Chaudhury, Dipanjan. 2017a. European MPs Caution OBOR Could Make Continent Subservient to China. *Economic Times*, May 6, Brussels.

———. 2017b. China May Hit Funds Roadblock Over OBOR, Think Tank Says. *Economic Times*, May 30, New Delhi.

Che, Pan. 2017. Survey Finds China Data Don't Show Full Picture of Overseas Shopping Spree. *Caixin Global*, August 24, Beijing.

Chen, Judy, et al. 2017. China's $162 Billion of Dealmaker Debt Raises Alarm. *Bloomberg News*, July 5, Hong Kong.

China Global Investment Tracker. 2017. *American Enterprise Institute*. Washington, DC: AEI.

China Investment Corp. 2015. *Annual Report*, Beijing.

China Money Network. 2014. *Anbang Insurance to Acquire Belgian Insurer Fidea from J.C. Flowers*, October 13. Retrieved from https://www.chinamoneynetwork.com/2014/10/13/anbang-insurance-to-acquire-belgian-insurer-fidea-from-j-c-flowers

Chu, Charlene. 2017. *Unproductive Credit Continues to Mount*. London: Autonomous Research. July 5.

Collier, Andrew. 2016. Interview, Orient Capital Research. September 12.

Cooley, Alexander. 2016. The Political Economy of OBOR. *CSIS*, October. Washington, DC.

Corman, David, et al. 2017. *A Pocket Guide to Chinese Cross-Border M&A*, 6. Shanghai: Mckinsey China.

Culi, Li, Sun and Xu. 2015. *Government Connections and Financial Constraints: Evidence from a Large Representative Sample of Chinese Firms*. International Finance Discussion Papers. Washington, DC: Federal Reserve. January.

Cull, Robert, Wei Li, Bo Sun, and Lixin Colin Xu. 2015. *Government Connections and Financial Constraints: Evidence from a Large Representative Sample of Chinese Firms*. International Finance Discussion Papers 1129. Washington, DC: Board of Governors of the Federal Reserve.

Dejong, Piter. 2017. Getting the Numbers Right on China's Actual Overseas Investment: The Case of the Netherlands. *Journal of Current Chinese Affairs* 46 (1): 187–209.

Dolan, Kerry A. 2017. Who Is the Chinese Tycoon That Donald Trump's Son-In-Law Met With? *Forbes*, January 9.

Dollar, David. 2015. *United States-China Two-Way Direct Investment: Opportunities and Challenges*. Washington, DC: John L. Thornton China Center, Brookings Institution.

———. 2017a. *Yes, China Is Investing Globally—But Not So Much in Its Belt and Road Initiative*. Washington, DC: Brookings Institution. May 8.

———. 2017b. *China's New Investment Rules*. Washington, DC: Brookings Institution. August 23.

European Council on Foreign Relations. 2015. *One Belt One Road: China's Great Leap Outward*. Paris: ECFR. June.

Evans, Nick. 2017. CITIC Flags Another $US1b Writedown on Sino Iron. *The West Australian*, February 16, Perth.

Forsythe, Michael. 2017. The Billionaire Gadfly in Exile Who Stared Down Beijing. *New York Times*, New York, May 30.

Forsythe, Michael, and Jonathan Ansfield. 2016. A Chinese Mystery: Who Owns a Firm on a Global Shopping Spree? *New York Times*, September 1.

Fun, Ho Wah. 2017. Asean Belt and Road Risks Under Scrutiny. *The Star Online*, July 30, Kuala Lumpur.

Gabriel Wildau. 2016. Rise of Wu Xiaohui, Anbang's Low-Profile, High-Octane Chairman. *Financial Times*, March 15.

Gadfly Exile Who Stared Down Beijing. *New York Times*, New York.

Gallagher, Kevin, Jose Ocampo, Ming Zhang, and Yongding Yu. 2014. *Capital Account Liberalization in China: A Cautionary Tale*. Boston University, Pardee Center for School of Global Studies, Policy Brief, Issue 002, July.

Gang, Fan. 2013. *The Role of State Owned Enterprises in the Chinese Economy*. U.S. China 2022. Hong Kong: China-United States Exchange Foundation.

Giorno, Guy. 2012. *Investment Canada Act: State-Owned Enterprise Policy*. Toronto: Fasken Martineau Institute. December 19.

Gloudeman, Lauren, and Nargiza Salidjanova. 2016. *Policy Considerations for Negotiating a U.S.-China Bilateral Investment Treaty*. Washington, DC: U.S.-China Economic and Security Review Commission. August 1.

Godemont, Francois. 2015. *One Belt One Road: China's Great Leap Outward*. European Council on Foreign Relations. Paris: ECFR.

Grassley, Charles. 2016. *Grassley Statement on Conclusion of CFIUS Review of ChemChina-Syngenta Merger*, August 22. Accessed at https://www.grassley.senate.gov/news/news-releases/grassley-statement-conclusion-cfius-review-chemchina-syngenta-merger

Hanemann, Thilo. 2017. *Tectonic Shifts: Chinese Outbound M&A in 1H 2017*. New York: Rhodium Group. June 27.

Huang, Kaixi, et al. 2016. *In Syngenta Bid, ChemChina Follows Buyout Formula*. Beijing: Caixin. November 13.

Hui-Yong, Yu. 2016. Blackstone Said to Sell Hotels to Anbang for $6.5 Billion. *Bloomberg*, March 12. Retrieved from https://www.bloomberg.com/news/articles/2016-03-12/blackstone-said-selling-strategic-hotels-to-anbang-for-6-5-bln

Hwang, Jyhjong. 2017. *Guest Post: Desert Mirage: Fact-checking China in Namibia*, May 9. Www.Chinaafricarealstory.com

IMF. 2014. International Financial Statistics. *China Outlook*. Washington, DC: IMF, December 20.

Interview, Orient Capital Research. 2016. Shanghai, June.

———. 2017. New York, May.

Interview with Orient Capital Research. 2017. June 11.

Lai, Wayne. 2017. *Heavy Reliance on Puttable Bonds Poses Funding Risks for Some Chinese Firms*. Fitch Ratings: Hong Kong. June 28.

Lam, Steven. 2017a. *Chinese Authorities Put the Squeeze on Anbang*. Bloomberg: Hong Kong. June 22.

Lam, Ka-Sing. 2017b. Chinese Buying of US Residential Property Hits Record High. *South China Morning Post*, July 19, Hong Kong.

Lardy, Nicholas. 2014. *Markets Over Mao*. Washington, DC: Peterson Institute.

Le Corre, Phillip. 2016. *China's Global Rise. Can the EU and the U.S. Pursue a Coordinated Strategy*. Washington, DC: Brookings Institution.

Le Corre, Philippe, and Alain Sepulchre. 2016. *China's Offensive in Europe (Geopolitics in the 21st Century)*. Washington, DC: Brookings.

Lehman, Lee and Xu. 2017. *How Much is the Permissible Debt to Equity of a Joint Venture*. China Knowledge International Perspective, online at www.lehmanlaw.com

Lelyveld, Michael. 2017. Chinese Investment Lags in Belt and Road Countries. *Eurasia Review*, August 1, Albany/Oregon.

Leng, Sydney. 2017. Beijing Claims Win Against 'Irrational' Outbound Cash, Stopping 'Crocodiles' and 'Ants' in Their Tracks. *SCMP*, August 2, Hong Kong.

Levine, Henry. 2017. Private Correspondence with the Author, August 18.

Lin, Li-Wen. 2017a. National Champions: Governance Change Through Globalization? *University of Pennsylvania Asian Law Review* 11 (1): Article 3.

———. 2017b. *A Network Anatomy of Chinese State-Owned Enterprises*. San Domenico di Fiesole: European University Institute, Robert Schuman Centre for Advanced Studies.

Mallawarachi, Bharatha. 2017. Sri Lanka, China Sign Long-Delayed $1.5 Billion Port Deal. *Reuters*, July 29, Colombo.

Martina, Michael. 2017. In China, the Party's Push for Influence Inside Foreign Firms Stirs Fears. *Reuters*, August 24, Beijing.

McCauley, Robert, and Tom Orlik. 2017. *One Belt, One Road Topic Primer*. Beijing: Bloomberg. May 11.

McCauley, Robert, et al. 2017. *Financial Deglobalisation in Banking*? Basel: BIS Working Papers, No. 650. Basel: BIS, June.

McGregor, James. 2012. *No Ancient Wisdom, No Followers*. Connecticut: Prospecta Press.

Michaels, Dave. 2017. Chicago Exchange Sale Looks Shaky as China Tensions Rise. *The Wall Street Journal*, August 27, Chicago.

Milhaupt, Curtis J. 2013. We Are the (National) Champions: Understanding the Mechanisms of State Capitalism in China. *Stanford Law Review* 65: 697.

Milhaupt, Curtis J., and Wentong Zheng. 2015. Beyond Ownership: State Capitalism and the Chinese Firm. *Georgetown Law Journal* 103: 665.

Nager, Adam. 2016. *Calling Out China's Mercantilism.* Washington, DC: International Economy.

New York Times. 2017. *The Billionaire*, May 30.

Norris, William J. 2016. *Chinese Economic Statecraft: Commercial Actors, Grand Strategy, and State Control.* Ithaca: Cornell University Press.

O'Neill, Sean. 2015. Nuclear Deal with China Is a Threat to National Security. *The Times*, October 16, London.

Orient Capital Research. 2010. Interview.

Orr and Cogman. 2017. *A Pocket Guide to Chinese Cross-Border M&A*, 6. China: McKinsey.

Picketty, Thomas. 2017. *Capital Accumulation, Private Property and Rising Inequality in China, 1978–2015.* Working Paper 23368. Cambridge, MA: National Bureau of Economic Research. April.

Probsting, Michael. 2014. China's Emergence as an Imperial Power. *New Politics*, XV-1, Summer, Brooklyn.

Reuters. 2016. ChemChina Setting Up $5 Billion Fund to Help Finance Syngenta Bid. *Reuters*, December 1, London.

Rosen, Kenneth. 2016. *Breaking Ground: Chinese Investment in U.S. Real Estate.* New York: Asia Society.

SAFE. 2017. China Supports Legitimate, Compliant Overseas Investment: Regulator. *State Administration of Foreign Exchange*, November 30, Beijing.

Schmidt, Blake 2017. *This Chinese Dealmaker Is Raising Billions from Shadow Loans.* Hong Kong: Bloomberg. August 25

Scissors, Derek. 2016. American Enterprise Institute, July 14.

SCMP. 2017. How Did a Small Chinese Airline Become the King of Acquisitions? Chinese Media Wonder—And Then Suddenly Don't. *SCMP*, April 25, Hong Kong.

Sender, Henny. 2017. Billionaire Anbang boss Wu Xiaohui Barred from Leaving China. *Financial Times*, June 2. London.

Shi, Ting. 2017. It's Extremely Important Whether the Destination Countries Have Good Relations with China or Not. In *Chinese Companies Wary of Political Risks of Xi's Belt and Road.* Hong Kong: Bloomberg.

Shuping, Niu, and David Stanway. 2016. China Citizens Protest ChemChina-Syngenta Deal Amid GMO Worries. *Reuters*, April 8, Beijing.

Sina Finance. 2015. 风口浪尖的安邦保险:内部构造窥探 钱从哪里来. *Anbang Insurance: Examining Internal Sources of Funds.* Retrieved from http://finance.sina.com.cn/money/insurance/bxyx/20150204/071921471733.shtml

South China Morning Post. 2017. HNA Shares Plunge After Fugitive Tycoon's Allegations. *SCMP*, April 24, Hong Kong.

Southern Weekend. 2014a. *Anbang's Key Person.* Guangzhou: Southern Weekend. January 10.

———. 2014b. *Anbang: Who Is the Real Control?* Guangzhou: Southern Weekend. January 5.

Stewart, Phil. 2007. U.S. Weighs Restricting Chinese Investment in Artificial Intelligence. *Reuters*, Washington, DC.

Strategy & Corporate Finance|Chinese Globalization. 2017. Copyright © McKinsey & Company Design contact: GCO NewMedia, April. www.mckinseychina.com

Tang, Frank. 2017. China Takes Harsher Tone Against Big Dealmakers, Alleging 'Asset Transfer'. *South China Morning Post*, July 19, Hong Kong.

Tiezzi, Shannon. 2014. China Urges Companies to 'Go Global'. *The Diplomat*, December 25, Washington, DC.

Wang, Bijun, and Huiyao Wang. 2014. Chinese Manufacturing Firms' Overseas Direct Investment: Patterns, Motivations and Challenges. *Tokyo, Japan: Asian Economic Policy Review* 9 (2): 227–249.

Wang, Junmin, et al. 2011. *The Rise of SASAC: Asset Management, Ownership Concentration, and Firm Performance in China's Capital Markets*, 258. Beijing: Management and Organization Review.

Wang, Hao, et al. 2017. *Shadow Banking: China's Dual-Track Interest Rate Liberalization.* Beijing: Tsinghua University School of Economics and Management.

Wei, Lingling. 2015. China Economic Plan Calls for Mergers, Public Listings By 2020. *Wall Street Journal*, September 7, Beijing.

———. 2016. China Issuing Strict Controls on Overseas Investment. *Wall Street Journal*, November 26, Beijing.

Weinland, Don. 2017. Chemchina Edges Closer to Sealing Syngenta Deal. *Financial Times*, May 31, London.

Wildau, Gabriel. 2017. China 'New Silk Road' Investment Falls in 2016. *Financial Times*, May 10, Shanghai.

Wu, Wendy. 2016. *China Moves to Limit State Firms' Investments Overseas to Stem Capital Flight. South ChinaMorning Post*, December 1, Hong Kong.

Xie, Heng. 2016. China Steps Up Mortgage Controls in Some Property Markets. *Bloomberg News*, November 29, Hong Kong.

Xuexing, Jiang. 2017. BOC's Overseas Lending Outgrows Domestic Loans. *China Daily*, March 23, Beijing.

Yang, Quailing. 2017. Who Was China's Fallen Insurance Regulator Xiang Junbo?. *Caixin*, April 11, Beijing.

Yu, Xie. 2017. China Closes off Most Loan Options to Wang Jianlin's Wanda. *South China Morning Post*, July 17, Hong Kong.

Zhou, Xiaochuan. 2016. Interview. *Caixin Magazine*, February 15, Beijing.

Zhu, Julia. 2017. China Sovereign Wealth Fund CIC Plans More U.S. Investments: Chairman. *Reuters*, January 16, Hong Kong.

Zhu, Levin. 2017a. *Zhu Rongji's Son: China Has Overbuilt Houses for 300 Million People*. Shanghai: Chinascope. July 12.

Index

A. Collier, *China Buys the World*,
https://doi.org/10.1007/978-981-10-7494-3

The manufacturer's authorised representative in the EU is Springer
Nature Customer Service Centre GmbH, Europaplatz 3, 69115 Heidelberg,
Germany. If you have any concerns regarding our products, please
contact ProductSafety@springernature.com

Printed and bound by CPI Group (UK) Ltd, Croydon, CR0 4YY
30/09/2026
02225466-0009